More No-More-Than-4 Ingredient Recipes

More No-More-Than-4 Ingredient Recipes

The Kitchen Klutzes' Cookbook

By Joy Gallagher Douglas

With cartoons by Lynn Johnston

Doubleday Canada Limited, Toronto

Canadian Cataloguing in Publication Data
Douglas, Joy Gallagher, 1927-
More no-more-than-4 ingredient recipes
ISBN 0-385-25266-8
1. Cookery. 2. Cookery — Humor. I. Johnston, Lynn,
1947-   II. Title.
TX714.D68 1990   641.5'12   C90-093666-5

Editorial, production and design: Maggie Reeves
Cover design by Tania Craan
Printed and bound in the USA

Published in Canada by
Doubleday Canada Limited
105 Bond Street
Toronto, Ontario
M5B 1Y3

To order a membership certificate in Kitchen Klutzes
United, send $5 (cheque, cash or money order), PRINTING
the name and complete address of the recipient, to:
Joy Douglas, 4-44 Jackson Street, St. Thomas, Ontario
N5P 2R9

Allow four to six weeks for delivery.

This book is lovingly dedicated to
the 12,000 Kitchen Klutzes who have shared
their hilarious goofs with me.

CONTENTS

WOT HOPPENED?

I didn't have potatoes
So I substituted rice;
I didn't have paprika
So I used another spice.

I didn't have tomato sauce;
I used tomato paste,
(A whole can, not a half can –
I don't believe in waste!)

A friend gave me the recipe,
She said you couldn't beat it –
There must be something wrong with her.
I couldn't even eat it!

Author Unknown

INTRODUCTION

I always knew there would be a sequel to "No-More-Than-Four Ingredient Recipes: A Cookbook for Kitchen Klutzes," published by Doubleday in 1988. In the first place, I still had hundreds of good recipes with four or fewer ingredients, and files full of klutzy stories just waiting to be told. And I had a feeling, now justified, that I would hear from many more klutzes once the book was published.

Membership in Kitchen Klutzes United, which I formed in 1977, now stands at more than 12,000 members. Over the years the big certificate has been awarded to female and male klutzes ranging in age from nine to 92-years-old in 28 countries throughout the world. We are a happy gang of kitchen bunglers whose motto is, "Sorry I burned the tossed salad," and whose official prayer is, "Grant me the serenity to accept the fact that I am a Kitchen Klutz; the courage to march into any potluck with my latest disaster borne proudly on a silver platter; and the wisdom to tell anyone who makes a snide remark to go stuff a green banana up his nose!"

Of the hundreds of letters I have received since the first book came out, I got the biggest charge from one from Carol DeC. (All klutzes in this book are identified by first name and last initial only.)

One morning Carol prepared a chuck roast for baking later. She put it on a large square of silver foil, smeared a can of cream of mushroom soup and an envelope of dry onion soup mix over it, and sealed the foil around the roast. Into the fridge it went.

Later, Carol took the roast out and put it into a 250°F/120°C oven for four hours, which is exactly what she should have done. Came dinner time.

Carol opened the foil package, and lo and behold, what she had been roasting for four hours was a chunk of watermelon!

In this book you will read dozens more of these stories, each one guaranteed to give you a laugh. And when your laughter dies down, try some of the recipes. I have eaten or prepared, at one time or another, every one of them. There are only three things not counted as ingredients: salt, pepper, or less than a cup of flour. I figure that everyone has salt and pepper around, and if you don't have the flour, a neighbor will.

One more thing – "if you can't repair it, don't despair it!" Everyone, even gourmet cooks, goofs occasionally in the kitchen. Chalk it up to experience (which really is the best teacher), go on with your life and don't make the same mistake twice.

Happy cooking!

Brunch

Let Margaret McD. tell it: "I was preparing a great breakfast for my guests. I always add grated Parmesan cheese to scrambled eggs. Everyone at the table dug in, but their faces told me something was wrong. I took a bite of my scrambled eggs — grit! By mistake I had sprinkled them with powdered cleanser. . . ."

COTTAGE CHEESE OMELET

Serve with bacon and toasted English muffins.

6	eggs	6
1 cup	creamed cottage cheese	250 mL
2 Tbsp	butter or margarine	25 mL
1 Tbsp	chopped parsley	15 mL

In medium bowl, combine eggs, cottage cheese, salt and pepper. Beat until fluffy. Heat butter in large broiler-proof frying pan. Pour in egg mixture and cook over low heat until firm and browned on bottom. Put under broiler until lightly browned on top. Cut into wedges and sprinkle with parsley.
Serves 4

BAKED MUSHROOM OMELET

Serve with link sausages and buttered toast.

1/2 lb	mushrooms, sliced	250 g
1/4 cup	butter or margarine	75 mL
8	eggs, beaten	8
1/4 tsp	rosemary	1 mL

In frying pan, sauté mushrooms in butter. Combine with eggs, rosemary, salt and pepper. Turn into buttered 8-inch (2L) square baking pan and bake in preheated 325°F (160°C) oven for 15 minutes, or just until eggs are set.
Serves 4

Linda S. cooked omelets one Sunday. She accidentally dropped a half cup of flour into the pan, and when the recipient took the first bite, a big cloud of flour enveloped her face.

EGGS-IN-A-PICTURE-FRAME

My granddaughter christened this dish when she was three.

4	slices bread	4
1/4 cup	butter or margarine	50 mL
4	eggs	4
	Crisp bacon strips	

Using a 2-1/2-inch (6 cm) cookie cutter, cut centers from bread slices. In medium skillet, melt butter or margarine and brown bread "frames" on one side. Turn slices; break egg into saucer and slip into the middle of each bread slice. Cook over low heat until eggs are set to taste. Serve with bacon.
Serves 4

BACON AND APPLES

Try this on a cold winter morning.

4	large tart apples	4
8	slices bacon	8
2 Tbsp	vegetable oil	25 mL
2 Tbsp	brown sugar	25 mL

Peel apples and cut into cubes. You should have about 4 cups (1000 mL). In a large frying pan, sauté bacon until crisp. Drain and set aside. Remove all but 2 Tbsp (25 mL) of grease from the frying pan. Add vegetable oil to frying pan. Add apples, sprinkle with brown sugar, and sauté uncovered, until apples are tender. Serve apples with bacon.
Serves 4

EASY CHEESE SOUFFLÉ

Mom used to make this for Saturday night supper.

1	can cream of celery soup	1
1 cup	shredded sharp cheese	250 mL
6	eggs, separated	6
2 Tbsp	chopped parsley	25 mL

In large saucepan, combine soup and cheese. Heat slowly, stirring occasionally, until cheese has melted. Remove from heat. In large bowl, beat egg whites until soft peaks form. In medium bowl, beat egg yolks until thick and lemon colored. Gradually stir in soup mixture. Fold this mixture gently into whites until no streaks of white remain. Pour mixture into ungreased 2-qt (2L) casserole. Bake in preheated 300°F (140°C) oven for about 1 hour, or until soufflé is puffed and golden. Garnish with parsley and serve immediately.
Serves 4

BASIL BAKED TOMATOES

Delicious with crisp bacon and toasted, buttered bagels.

4	large firm tomatoes	4
4	eggs	4
2 Tbsp	grated cheese	25 mL
1 tsp	basil	5 mL

In medium saucepan, bring water to a boil. Scald the tomatoes in the boiling water for about 1 minute; remove skins. Cut a hollow center in each tomato and drop a whole raw egg in each. Sprinkle the top with salt, pepper, cheese and basil. Place in a shallow buttered baking dish and bake in preheated 350°F (180°C) oven for about 20 minutes.
Serves 4

OYSTERS AND EGGS

A gallant bachelor once served this at a delightful brunch.

8	eggs	8
1	small tin smoked oysters, drained and oil set aside	1
1 Tbsp	chopped parsley	15 mL

In medium bowl, beat eggs lightly. Add salt and pepper and mix. In a medium frying pan, add the oil from the oysters. Heat over low heat until the frying pan is hot, then remove excess oil. Add eggs to frying pan and scramble until half done. Add the oysters and continue scrambling until eggs are set to your satisfaction. Garnish with parsley.
Serves 4

SWEDISH EGGS

These go by many names and are good whatever they're called.

9	eggs	9
1 lb	bulk sausage meat	500 g
1 cup	fine dried bread crumbs	250 mL
1 qt	fat for deep frying	1 L

Hard cook 8 of the eggs. Separate remaining egg, and store the yolk for some other purpose. Slightly beat the egg white. Brush shelled eggs with egg white and cover each with sausage meat. Dip in egg white, then in bread crumbs. Fry in deep hot fat until brown, about 2 minutes. Cut into halves lengthwise. Serve hot.
Serves 6 to 8

Sally L. says she's not bad in the kitchen, but her uncle Ron is a disaster. "He's the only person I know who thought he was frying potatoes for breakfast and didn't realize it was potato salad until he bit into a radish."

HASH AND EGGS

Leftover homemade hash may be used instead of canned hash.

1	can (15-1/2 oz/500 mL) corned beef hash	1
1 Tbsp	oil	15 mL
6	eggs	6
1 Tbsp	chopped chives or parsley	15 mL

Remove both ends from canned hash, slide out hash and cut into 6 slices. Make a hollow in the center of each. In medium fry pan, sauté hash, hollowed side up, in oil until bottom is lightly browned. Break egg into saucer and slip one into each hollow. Sprinkle with salt and pepper and chives (or garnish finished dish with parsley). Cover and cook until eggs are done to taste.
Serves 6

ULTRA FRENCH TOAST

If you don't have self-rising flour, you will have to add 1-1/2 tsp (8 mL) baking powder and 1/2 tsp (2 mL) salt to the flour.

1 cup	self-rising flour	250 mL
1 cup	milk	250 mL
2	eggs, well beaten	2
8	slices raisin bread, cut into thirds	8

In large bowl, add flour. Add milk gradually, stirring constantly, until smooth. Beat in eggs. Cut each bread slice into thirds. Dip strips in batter and fry in greased frying pan until golden on both sides. Remove and place in shallow pan in warm oven until all are cooked.
Serves 6

MARNIE'S FRENCH TOAST

Don't substitute anything for the bacon fat — it makes the dish.

2	eggs	2
1/2 cup	milk	100 mL
6	slices bread	6
1/4 cup	bacon fat	50 mL

In small bowl, beat eggs, salt to taste, and milk. Dip bread into egg mixture, coating well on both sides. Melt bacon dripping in large frying pan. Sauté bread slices until golden on both sides.
Serves 3 to 4

COTTAGE CHEESE PANCAKES

Good served with hot applesauce as a topping.

6	eggs	6
1-1/2 cups	creamed cottage cheese	375 mL
1/2 cup	flour	125 mL
1/4 tsp	cinnamon	1 mL

In blender container or small bowl of mixer, beat eggs and cheese until smooth. Gradually add flour, salt and cinnamon. Mix until well blended. Pour batter by scant 1/4 (75 mL) cupfuls and separate 2 inches (5 cm) apart onto lightly greased hot griddle or frying pan. Cook on both sides until golden, turning once.
Serves 4

According to Nancy T: "We were making blueberry pancakes on one of those electric griddles on the counter, and the plastic bowl of batter was on top of one of the stove's elements. The next thing I remember is the pancake batter disappearing before our eyes, from the BOTTOM of the bowl. . . ."

BASIC PANCAKES OR CRÊPES

You can fill these with anything from strawberries to crabmeat.

2	large eggs	2
1/2 cup	sifted flour	125 mL
1 cup	milk	250 mL
	Filling	

In small mixing bowl, break eggs. Add flour and beat slowly but thoroughly. Add a pinch of salt and gradually beat in milk, beating slowly to keep the mixture from getting frothy. Put frying pan on high heat, grease bottom well. When pan is hot, pour in about 1/4 cup (50 mL) batter. Quickly swirl pan to coat bottom evenly with thin layer. Be ready to loosen it almost immediately. Turn pancake over and cook for a few seconds on the other side until golden brown. Turn out on a warmed plate and fill as desired. Roll up and serve.
Serves 4

SAUCED POTATO CAKES

A quick and easy breakfast dish.

1	envelope (3 oz/85 g) potato pancake mix	1
1 cup	chopped canned luncheon meat	250 mL
	Hot applesauce	

Prepare pancake mix, using milk as called for in directions. To batter, add chopped luncheon meat. For each pancake, drop about 2 Tbsp (25 mL) batter onto hot greased griddle or frying pan. Cook until golden brown on both sides, turning once. Serve with hot applesauce.
Serves 4

Appetizers & Soups

Virginia was mixing batter with a portable electric mixer. The cord came unplugged from the mixer and dropped into the batter. She fished it out and absent-mindedly proceeded to put the end in her mouth to lick off the batter, wondering all the while why her tongue was so tingly.

CHEESE BALLS

A melt-in-your-mouth, easy-to-do treat.

1 tsp	flour	5 mL
1 cup	grated sharp cheddar cheese	250 mL
1	egg white, stiffly beaten	1
1 qt	fat for deep frying	1 L

In medium bowl, mix 1/2 tsp (2 mL) salt and pepper to taste with flour and cheese. Fold in stiffly beaten egg white. Form into 1-inch (2.5 cm) balls and fry in deep hot fat (375°F/190°C) for about 5 minutes. Drain on absorbent paper.
Makes 24

SAUCY SHRIMP

This recipe can easily be doubled or tripled for a larger party.

1 cup	chili sauce	250 mL
1 cup	pickle relish	250 mL
1 cup	beer	250 mL
2 cups	small cleaned shrimp	500 mL

In medium saucepan, combine chili sauce, pickle relish and beer. Place on high heat for 3–4 minutes, stirring once. Reduce heat to medium and continue cooking for about 10 minutes, or until sauce thickens, stirring occasionally. Add shrimp and cook on high heat just until shrimp are pink and tender. Cover and let stand two minutes. Serve on small platter with toothpicks.
Serves 4

MUSHROOMS CAREEN

Careen Collins says you have to use your own judgement on the amounts of sherry, butter and caviar, depending on the size of the mushrooms.

        Large mushroom caps
        Sherry
        Butter
        Caviar

Remove stems from mushrooms so that a nice indention is left. Put a bit of sherry and butter in each cap, and broil 3 inches (7.5 cm) from source of heat until mushrooms are tender, about 5–6 minutes. Allow to cool, then fill caps with caviar.

WATER CHESTNUT WONDERS

These have a marvelous, crunchy tang.

3 cups	drained water chestnuts	750 mL
1/4 cup	soy sauce	50 mL
6	bacon slices, cut into quarters	6
1/4 cup	sugar	50 mL

In large covered bowl, marinate water chestnuts in soy sauce for at least 30 minutes (overnight is even better). Cut bacon slices in quarters. Roll water chestnuts in sugar, then in bacon. Secure with toothpicks. Bake in preheated 400°F (200°C) oven for 20 minutes. May be reheated in 350°F (180°C) oven for 10 minutes. Makes a nice large tray of appetizers.
Makes 3 cups (750 mL)

JAMAICA DIP

"Jamaica dip? Yes, and here's how I did it!"

2	ripe avocados	2
3 tsp	lemon juice	15 mL
2 Tbsp	onion juice	25 mL
1/2 cup	dairy sour cream	125 mL

In small mixing bowl, mash avocados with lemon and onion juices, and salt to taste. Blend in sour cream. This is an excellent dip for large potato chips.
Makes about 2 cups (500 mL)

CLAM CROWDER

This recipe comes from an old friend, Molly Crowder.

2 cups	minced clams, drained	500 mL
1	package (8 oz/227 g) cream cheese, softened	1
	Hot pepper sauce, to taste	
	Lemon juice, to taste	

In small bowl, mix all ingredients plus salt to taste. Heat in double boiler or chafing dish. Good with melba toast.
Serves 4

Catherine B. tells us about her klutzy husband, Morgan. "He was supposed to be making breaded chicken balls with pineapple sauce," she says. "But he had mixed the batter of flour, eggs, seasonings and water, and dumped the pineapple sauce, which was supposed to go over the finished product, into the batter. What a mess — and I couldn't convince him he was wrong."

LITTLE CHEESE PIZZAS

Leftovers may be stored in the refrigerator for up to four days, and may be reheated.

1	package (10) refrigerated biscuits (dough)	1
1 cup	spaghetti sauce	250 mL
1 cup	grated mozzarella cheese	250 mL
	Oregano to taste	

On a greased metal baking sheet using the floured bottom of a glass, flatten each biscuit to a 4-inch (10 cm) circle, forming a ridge around the edge. Spread with spaghetti sauce, then sprinkle with cheese and oregano. Bake in preheated 425°F (220°C) oven for about 10 minutes, or until edges are lightly browned.
Makes 10

PARMESAN RICE SQUARES

A lovely way to eat your cereal.

2 cups	bite-size crisp rice squares	500 mL
3 Tbsp	butter, melted	45 mL
1/4 cup	grated fresh Parmesan cheese	50 mL
Pinch	paprika	Pinch

In shallow pan, toss rice squares in butter until coated. Sprinkle with cheese and paprika. Toast in 300°F (140°C) oven about 15 minutes, stirring occasionally. Allow to cool.
Makes 2 cups (500 mL)

HOT ARTICHOKE DIP

Use the water-packed artichoke hearts for this recipe, not the marinated ones.

1	can (14 oz/398 g) artichoke hearts, drained and chopped	1
1 cup	mayonnaise (not salad dressing)	250 mL
1/2 cup	grated fresh Parmesan cheese	125 mL
Pinch	paprika	Pinch

In small bowl, mix mayonnaise and cheese thoroughly. Stir in chopped artichoke hearts. Place in a small ovenproof dish and sprinkle with paprika. Bake in preheated 350°F (180°C) oven for about 20 minutes, or until lightly browned and bubbly. Serve as a dip with raw veggies, or use as a spread on unsalted crackers or pumpernickel bread fingers.
Makes about 2 cups (500 mL)

FAKE DE FOIE GRAS

They'll never know it's not the expensive, imported kind!

1/2 lb	liver sausage	250 g
1/2 cup	mayonnaise	125 mL
	Juice from half a lemon	

Remove skin from liver sausage and, in a small bowl, mash with a fork until smooth. Mix in other ingredients. Chill. Serve with crackers.
Makes about 1-1/2 cups (375 mL)

RITA'S RICOTTA DIP

Rita says not to use a blender or food processor for this recipe, since it will destroy the texture of the cheese.

2 cups	ricotta cheese, at room temperature	500 mL
4 oz	(1/2 cup) cream cheese, softened	125 mL
2–3	cloves garlic, crushed	2–3
1/4 cup	finely chopped fresh parsley	50 mL

In small bowl, combine all ingredients. Add salt and freshly ground pepper to taste and mix by hand thoroughly. Cover bowl with plastic wrap and refrigerate at least 2 hours; longer is better.
Makes about 2-1/2 cups (625 mL)

CURRIED YOGURT DIP

Diet tip: This is relatively low in calories.

2/3 cup	plain low-fat yogurt	150 mL
1/3 cup	dairy sour cream	75 mL
1 Tbsp	curry powder, or to taste	15 mL
1 tsp	lemon juice	5 mL

In small bowl, combine all ingredients and salt and pepper to taste. Cover and refrigerate for an hour or more.
Makes about 1 cup (125 mL)

Writes Marianna O'G., "Rhonda and her father prepared deviled eggs by emptying out the yolks, filling the little depressions with plain mayonnaise, then complaining they couldn't eat another yolk."

BACON-CHEESE DIP

My granddaughter loves this with carrot sticks.

4	slices bacon, diced	4
1	package (8 oz/227 g) cream cheese	1
1/4 cup	sweet-sour salad dressing	50 mL
2 Tbsp	milk	25 mL

In small frying pan, sauté bacon until crisp. Place on paper towels to drain. Combine cream cheese, salad dressing and milk in a medium bowl, and beat until smooth. Fold in bacon. Chill for several hours.
Makes about 1 cup (250 mL)

CHICKEN MORSELS

A gourmet cooking student in Toronto passed this recipe to me. Be sure the chicken is finely ground.

1 cup	finely ground cooked chicken	250 mL
1 tsp	curry powder	5 mL
3 Tbsp	chutney syrup	45 mL
1/2 cup	minced parsley	125 mL

In small bowl, mix all ingredients except parsley and form into walnut-size balls. Coat with parsley. Chill and serve with toothpicks.
Makes 16-20

David S. decided to make guacamole. The recipe called for three or four cloves of garlic. "I thought that a clove of garlic was the entire bulb," he said, "so I put in four whole bulbs. Then I decided to double the recipe, so I put in four more. Now, since it takes garlic a while to permeate

COCONUT BALLS

These are pretty speared with colored toothpicks.

1	package (8 oz/227 g) cream cheese, softened	1
1-1/2 Tbsp	chopped chutney	20 mL
1 tsp	curry powder	5 mL
1/2 cup	flaked coconut	125 mL

In small bowl, mix all ingredients except coconut. Chill slightly, then form into bite-sized balls and roll in coconut.
Makes 36

GINGERY STUFFED CELERY

Even children go for these.

1	package (3 oz/85 g) cream cheese, softened	1
1/2 cup	raisins, finely chopped	125 mL
1/4 tsp	ground ginger	1 mL
6	large ribs celery, about 9 inches (22.5 cm) long	6

In small bowl, combine cream cheese, raisins and ginger and mix well. Spread in hollow of celery ribs. Cut into 1-inch (2.5 cm) pieces.
Makes about 54

---

thoroughly, and since the recipe was so good, I managed to consume a lot of it within a short period of time without noticing how strong it was. Everything was fine until about 2:00 A.M. when I woke up to the odor of garlic coming from my body, and couldn't get back to sleep. The next four days I remained in the house and cancelled all my appointments — the odor was so bad that even my cat wouldn't come close to me!"

CURRIED POTATO-APPLE SOUP

A marvelous first course for a ladies' luncheon.

1	can (10-1/2 oz/300 g) cream of potato soup	1
1	soup can milk	1
1	apple, quartered, peeled and cored	1
1/2 tsp	curry powder	2 mL

In blender container, combine all ingredients and whirl until smooth. Turn into small saucepan and heat gently over low heat.
Serves 4

SPLIT PEA SOUP

Watch the salt — if the ham is salty, you won't need to add any.

1	ham bone with meat	1
1 lb	green split peas, washed	500 g
1	carrot, finely diced	1
1	small onion, finely diced	1

Put ham bone in kettle with 2 to 3 qts (2 to 3 L) water. Bring to a boil, cover and simmer for about 90 minutes, or until meat falls off bone. Discard bone. Add split peas to soup, cover and simmer for 1 hour longer, or until peas are cooked into a purée, stirring occasionally. Add carrot and onion and cook another 20 minutes, or until tender. Just before serving, season with freshly ground black pepper and additional salt, if needed.
Serves 6

OYSTER SOUP

This was traditionally served on Christmas Eve at our house when I was growing up.

1 pint	oysters	500 mL
6 Tbsp	butter	90 mL
1 qt	milk	1 L
Pinch	nutmeg	Pinch

Make sure oysters are free from bits of shell. In saucepan, melt butter. Add oysters and their liquid and cook just until edges of oysters curl, 1 to 2 minutes. Add milk, 1-1/2 tsp (7 mL) salt and 1/8 tsp (0.5 mL) pepper, and nutmeg. Bring almost to the boiling point but do not boil.
Serves 4

LENTIL SOUP

You can use almost any kind of lentil for this soup. I like to use either pinto or navy beans.

1 cup	lentils	125 mL
1/2 lb	link sausages, cut into bite-size pieces	250 g
1/2 cup	presifted flour	125 mL

The day before you plan to make the soup, cover the lentils in a pot with water and let soak. The next day, drain lentils and put back into pot with 1 qt (1 L) cold water. Bring to a boil, cover and simmer for 1 hour. Add sausages and simmer 1 hour longer. In skillet, brown flour until golden. Add 1/2 cup (125 mL) water. Mix and put into soup. Stir until soup is thick. Season with salt and freshly ground black pepper.
Serves 4

EGG DROP SOUP

One of two traditional Chinese soups (also see Won Ton Soup below).

1-1/2 qts	chicken broth	1.5 L
1/2 cup	diced cooked ham	125 mL
1/4 cup	sliced green onions	50 mL
1	egg, slightly beaten	1

In large saucepan, bring chicken broth to a boil. Add ham and onions. Return to boiling. Remove from heat. Slowly pour in egg, using a circular, stirring motion.
Serves 6

WON TON SOUP

The perfect start for a chow mein dinner.

1-1/2 qts	chicken broth	1.5 L
24	frozen won tons, thawed	24
2 Tbsp	chopped scallions or green onions	25 mL
2 Tbsp	soy sauce	25 mL

In large saucepan, bring chicken broth to a boil. Arrange four won tons each in six soup bowls. Sprinkle each with scallions and soy sauce. Pour boiling broth into bowls and serve at once.
Serves 6

"My problem was not knowing what happens to barley when it cooks," says Yvonne R. "For a 2-quart (2 L) pot of beef and barley soup, a cup of barley didn't seem like very much, so I put in two cups. Now, there was a soup you could really eat with a fork. . . ."

SPINACH-MUSHROOM SOUP

An unusual soup children hate and adults love, so be fore-warned!

2 lbs	fresh spinach	1 kg
2	cans (10-1/2 oz/300 g each) condensed cream of mushroom soup	2
3	soup cans half and half cream	3
Pinch	nutmeg	Pinch

Wash spinach. In large pot, steam spinach in the water that clings to it until well wilted. Drain well. Blend spinach, soup and half and half cream. Heat gently. Sprinkle with nutmeg.
Serves 8

PARTY SQUASH SOUP

This will be a hit at your next winter dinner party!

6	very small acorn squash	6
2 cups	chicken stock or rich broth	500 mL
3 cups	heavy cream	750 mL
Pinch	nutmeg	Pinch

Cut tops off squash (as for jack-o-lantern); set aside to use as lids. Scoop out seeds. Cut enough off bottom so that it will sit flat, being careful not to make a hole in the bottom. Fill squash with 1/3 cup (75 mL) chicken broth and 2/3 cup (150 mL) cream each. Sprinkle each with nutmeg, salt and pepper. Cover with lid and wrap in aluminum foil. Bake in preheated 350°F (180°C) oven for 1 hour.
Serves 6

CRABMEAT BISQUE

If you want to be real elegant, add 4 Tbsp (60 mL) sherry when you add the crabmeat. Ooh, la la!

1	can (10-1/2 oz/300 g) cream of mushroom soup	1
1	can (10-1/2 oz/300 g) cream of asparagus soup	1
1-1/2 cups	milk	375 mL
1	can (6 oz/170 g) crabmeat, drained and flaked	1

In large saucepan, combine soups and milk and blend thoroughly. Add crabmeat and heat but do not boil.
Serves 6

AVOCADO CREAM SOUP

Avocado lovers will rave over this one.

1	large ripe avocado, peeled and quartered	1
1	can (10-1/2 oz/300 g) cream of chicken soup	1
1	soup can milk or half and half cream	1
Pinch	chili powder	Pinch

Peel and quarter the avocado, removing seed. In blender container, add soup and milk; cover and blend until smooth. With blender running, remove center cap from lid and add avocado. Blend only until avocado is coarsely chopped. Pour into a saucepan and heat gently over low heat. Stir in chili powder. Serve immediately.
Serves 4

EASY BROCCOLI CHOWDER

Even broccoli-hating children like this chowder.

1	package dry cream of celery soup mix	1
2 cups	fresh chopped broccoli	500 mL
1/2 cup	half and half cream	125 mL
Pinch	nutmeg	Pinch

In small saucepan, add dry cream of celery soup mix. Stir in 3 cups (750 mL) cold water gradually and bring to a boil, stirring constantly. Partially cover and simmer for 10 minutes. Add broccoli and cream. Heat, stirring constantly. Sprinkle with nutmeg.
Serves 4

HURRY-UP MUSHROOM SOUP

You'll never know this started with a can of Old Reliable.

1	can (10-1/2 oz/300 g) cream of mushroom soup	1
1	can (10 oz/284 g) mushrooms, drained	1
3/4 cup	evaporated milk	175 mL
1/2 cup	white wine	125 mL

In medium saucepan, combine all ingredients. Heat gently but thoroughly. Pour into bowls and serve.
Serves 4

Debra S. started a Christmas Eve tradition at their home: big bowls of homemade clam chowder. She followed the recipe carefully and made only one small mistake — she used sweetened condensed milk instead of evaporated milk. "Well," says her husband, Grant, "it was a disaster. The story has become a tradition in our home, even if the recipe will never be handed down!"

GERMAN CABBAGE SOUP

This takes a while to prepare, but it's worth it.

3 lbs	cabbage, finely shredded	1.5 kg
1/2 lb	butter	250 g
2 Tbsp	sugar	25 mL
3	cans beef consommé	3

Finely shred the cabbage. In heavy saucepan, melt the butter and add cabbage. Stir cabbage until it is coated well with butter. Sprinkle with sugar and cook over low heat for 45 minutes to 1 hour, or until cabbage is brown. Add consommé and 3 cans water (or 9 cups/2 L beef stock may be used), 1 tsp (5 mL) salt and 1/2 tsp (2 mL) pepper. Cover and cook over low heat for 2 hours.
Serves 8 generously

CHICKEN-RICE SOUP

If you don't have chicken broth, use 4 chicken bouillon cubes and a little less than 4 cups (1 L) hot water.

4 cups	chicken broth	1 L
1-1/2 cups	cooked rice or precooked rice	375 mL
3/4 cup	chopped cooked spinach	175 mL
1/4 cup	grated Parmesan cheese	50 mL

In large saucepan, put chicken broth. Add rice and spinach. Bring to a boil over low heat. Season with salt and pepper and serve hot sprinkled with grated cheese.
Serves 4

Casseroles and Pasta

Three-year-old Joey B. is well on his way to being an accomplished Kitchen Klutz. Stopping to answer the phone while grinding items for a meatloaf, Joey's mother Linda left him coloring a picture on the other side of the table. Joey proceeded to feed several brightly colored crayons into the meatloaf mixture — a fact she didn't know until after it was baked. . . .

EASY SAUSAGE LOAF

Serve with baked apples and hot fluffy rice.

2 lbs	bulk pork sausage	1 kg
4 cups	fresh bread crumbs	1 L
1	egg	1
1 cup	dairy sour cream	125 mL

Combine all ingredients (and 1/2 tsp/2 mL paprika if you like) and pack mixture into an ungreased 2-qt (2 L) loaf pan. Bake in preheated 350°F (180°C) oven for 1-1/2 hours.
Serves 6

SAUSAGE-STUFFED SQUASH

An inexpensive dinner dish.

2	acorn squash	2
1 lb	bulk pork sausage	500 g
1	small onion, grated	1
1-1/2 cups	soft bread crumbs	375 mL

Cut squash in half and remove seeds. Place cut side down in covered baking pan with 1/2 inch (1 cm) of boiling water in the bottom, and bake in 400°F (200°C) oven until squash is tender. Meanwhile, in frying pan, mash sausage with a fork and fry until cooked but not brown. Drain off fat. Add onion, bread crumbs, 1 tsp (5 mL) salt and 1/8 tsp (0.5 mL) pepper to sausage. Fill centers of squash halves with mixture. Reduce oven heat to 350°F (180°C) and bake, uncovered, for about 30 minutes longer.
Serves 4

KIELBASA AND SAUERKRAUT

Go-alongs: baked potatoes and green peas.

1	can (27 oz/775 g) sauerkraut, drained	1
1/2 tsp	celery seeds	2 mL
1 lb	Kielbasa (Polish sausage)	500 g
3 Tbsp	brown sugar	45 mL

In a 6-cup (1.5 L) baking dish, mix sauerkraut with celery seeds. Remove casing from sausage and make several deep cuts, 1-inch (2.5 cm) apart, in the meat; push sausage halfway down into sauerkraut. In a 1 cup (250 mL) measure, dissolve brown sugar in 1/2 cup (125 mL) hot water; drizzle over the sausage and sauerkraut. Cover and bake in preheated 350°F (180°C) oven for 1 hour, or until sausage is tender and sauerkraut is heated through.
Serves 4

KIELBASA AND CABBAGE

My friend Rheita Hughes, who is of Polish heritage, taught me to make this many years ago when we were college roomies.

1 lb	cooked Kielbasa, thinly sliced	500 g
1	medium onion, chopped	1
2 Tbsp	butter or margarine	25 mL
6 cups	(about 1 lb/500 g) shredded cabbage	1.5 L

In large frying pan, brown kielbasa and onion in butter or margarine. Add cabbage, 2 Tbsp (25 mL) water and 1 tsp (5 mL) salt. Cover and simmer until cabbage is tender, about 10 minutes, stirring occasionally.
Serves 4

HAM AND NOODLES

Those packaged noodle and sauce mixtures can come in handy.

1	package (4-1/2 oz/126 g) noodles Romanoff mix	1
1-1/2 cups	cooked ham, cut into strips	375 mL
1	can (8 oz/227 g) cut green beans	1
2 Tbsp	chopped pimiento	25 mL

Prepare noodle mix as directed on package, but increase milk to 2/3 cup (150 mL). (I know this is breaking the 4-ingredient rule, but pretend you didn't notice!) Add ham, beans and pimiento. Turn into a 1-1/2-qt (1.5 L) casserole and bake in preheated 350°F (180°C) oven for 20 minutes.
Serves 3

SALMON AND NOODLES

This one is legitimate!

1	package (4-1/2 oz/126 g) noodles Romanoff mix	1
1	can (8 oz/227 g) salmon	1
1/2 cup	cottage cheese	125 mL

Prepare noodle mix as directed on package, but increase milk to 2/3 cup (150 mL). (See, this time we're counting the milk as the fourth ingredient!) Stir in salmon and cheese. Turn into a greased 1-qt (1 L) casserole, cover and bake in preheated 350°F (180°C) oven for 20 minutes.
Serves 3

BARBECUED RIBS AND BEANS

Go-alongs: waldorf salad and broccoli with cheese sauce.

4 lbs	spareribs, cut into serving pieces	2 kg
2	cans (1 lb/500 g each) large lima beans	2
1 cup	barbecue sauce	250 mL

In a large pot, cover spareribs with water. Bring to a boil, reduce heat and simmer 1 hour, or until ribs are tender. Drain. Put ribs in shallow roasting pan and cover with 3/4 cup (175 mL) of the barbecue sauce. Then put beans in center of ribs and cover with remaining barbecue sauce. Bake in preheated 375°F (190°C) oven for about 30 minutes, or until glazed, basting with the sauce if necessary.
Serves 4 to 6

BAKED RIBS WITH BEANS

Serve with pineapple slices sautéed in a little butter and brown sugar.

| 3 lbs | spareribs, cut into serving pieces | 1.5 kg |
| 1 | can (28 oz/795 g) pork and beans in tomato sauce | 1 |

In roasting pan, place ribs and sprinkle with salt and pepper. Add 1/2 cup (125 mL) hot water. Cover and bake in preheated 350°F (180°C) oven for 2 hours. Uncover and bake 30 minutes. Add beans and bake 30 minutes more, or until ribs are done and beans are heated.
Serves 4

FISH-HOUSE HASH

Great with corn-on-the-cob and sliced tomatoes.

1/4 lb	salt pork, diced small	125 g
1	medium onion, chopped	1
2 cups	boiled potatoes, diced	500 mL
2 cups	flaked cooked fish	500 mL

In a hot frying pan, cook the salt pork until fat is rendered and
bits of pork are brown and crisp. Remove, drain on paper toweling and set aside. In medium bowl, toss together the onion,
potatoes, fish, and salt and pepper to taste (go easy on the salt;
the pork is salty). Stir this mixture into the fat in the frying
pan and cook over medium heat. Press down with the bottom of
a spatula and cook about 6 minutes, or until the bottom is
browned. Turn and brown other side. Turn out onto a heated
platter and sprinkle with the bits of salt pork.
Serves 4

HOT SAUSAGE AND VEGETABLES

Sweet Italian sausages may be substituted.

1 lb	hot Italian sausages	500 g
1/2 cup	chopped celery	125 mL
1	package (10 oz/284 g) frozen baby lima beans	1
2	cans (12 oz/340 g each) whole kernel corn with sweet peppers	2

Cut sausages into 1/2-inch (1 cm) slices and brown in a large
frying pan for about 15 minutes. Push sausages to one side,
add celery and sauté until celery is soft. Stir in lima beans and
corn. Simmer for 10 minutes, or until heated through.
Serves 4

HAM DINNER DISH

This is practically a meal in itself.

1	package (7-1/4 oz/205 g) macaroni-cheese dinner	1
1-1/2 cups	julienne-cut cooked ham	375 mL
1	can (8 oz/227 g) peas and carrots, drained	1
1/4 cup	milk	50 mL

Prepare macaroni-cheese dinner according to package directions. Stir in ham and peas and carrots. Add milk. Heat thoroughly over low heat.
Serves 4

HAM HOCK DINNER

You can add a small head of cabbage, quartered, 15 minutes before cooking is finished.

2 lbs	smoked ham hocks	1 kg
4	medium carrots, scraped	4
4	medium onions, peeled and halved	4
4	medium potatoes, peeled	4

In deep pot, cook ham hocks in water to cover for 2 hours. When they have cooked 1-1/2 hours, remove and discard skins from hocks. Return hocks to pot and add carrots, onions and potatoes. Cook 30 minutes longer, or until meat and vegetables are tender.
Serves 4

FRUIT MEAT LOAF

The applesauce gives it a great tang.

1-1/2 lbs	ground beef	1.5 kg
3/4 cup	fine bread crumbs	175 mL
3/4 cup	applesauce	175 mL
6 Tbsp	catsup	90 mL

In large bowl, combine all ingredients. Mix lightly with fork and form into a 6-inch (15 cm) square in a greased baking pan. Bake in preheated 350°F (180°C) oven for about 50 minutes.
Serves 6

EGGPLANT-BEEF CASSEROLE

I was served this at a luncheon in Savannah, Georgia.

1	medium eggplant, peeled and sliced	1
1-1/2 lbs	ground round steak	1.5 kg
1-1/2 cups	tomato sauce	375 mL
1/4 cup	grated fresh Parmesan cheese	50 mL

In a well-buttered 2-qt (2 L) casserole, add sliced eggplant. Cover with the meat and then with the tomato sauce. Bake in preheated 350°F (180°C) oven for 1 hour. Sprinkle with grated Parmesan cheese.
Serves 6

Nancy T. tells of her friend, Janet L. "Janet is deserving of your Kitchen Klutz Award for her now famous Meatloaf Soup. As far as she can recall, it was made with one part meat and three parts liquid. She literally poured dinner onto the table!"

DOUBLE BEEFY MEAT LOAF

Try this with broccoli and potatoes au gratin.

1 lb	ground beef	500 g
2 Tbsp	instant minced onion	25 mL
3/4 cup	saltine cracker crumbs	175 mL
	(about 18 crackers)	
1	can (10-1/2 oz/298 g) beef broth	1

Combine beef, onion, cracker crumbs and a pinch of pepper.
Mix well. Add beef broth and mix until thoroughly blended.
Turn into a greased 1-qt (1 L) loaf pan and bake in preheated
350°F (180°C) oven for about 45 minutes.
Serves 4

SAUCY MEAT LOAF

Go-alongs: brussels sprouts and canned sliced peaches.

1	large onion, sliced	1
1-1/2 lbs	ground beef	1.5 kg
1/2 tsp	basil	2 mL
1	can (10-1/2 oz/298 g) tomato with	1
	rice soup	

Save 3 onion rings for topping. Place the rest of the onion slices
in the bottom of an 8-inch (2 L) square baking pan. Cover
onions with ground beef; break up lightly with a fork but do not
pack down. Sprinkle with salt and basil and top with reserved
onion rings. Pour tomato with rice soup over all. Bake in
preheated 375°F (190°C) oven for 45 minutes.
Serves 4 to 6

GRANNY'S CASSEROLE

This is a great way to use up Easter's hard-cooked eggs.

1	can (14 oz/398 g) seasoned green beans, drained	1
1	can (10-1/2 oz/298 g) cream of mushroom soup	1
3	hard cooked eggs, chopped	3
1/2 cup	(6 slices) bacon, cooked and crumbled	125 mL

In greased 1-qt (1 L) casserole, combine drained green beans with undiluted soup. Fold in chopped eggs. Bake in preheated 375°F (190°C) oven about 40 to 45 minutes. Top with crumbled bacon.
Serves 4 to 6

CABBAGE-GREEN BEAN CASSEROLE

This is good served with chicken or ham.

2 cups	finely chopped green cabbage	500 mL
2	packages (10 oz/284 g each) frozen frenched green beans	2
1	can (10-1/2 oz/298 g) cheddar cheese soup	1
1 cup	buttered bread crumbs	250 mL

In medium saucepan, cook cabbage in water to cover for 5 minutes; drain. Cook frozen beans in same manner; drain. Mix cabbage and green beans with undiluted soup and pour into buttered 2-qt (2 L) casserole. Top with buttered bread crumbs (or a can of french fried onions). Bake at 350°F (180°C) until mixture bubbles.
Serves 6 to 8

STEAK-ARTICHOKE CASSEROLE

The next time someone gives you some Jerusalem artichokes, and you don't know what to do with them, do the following:

1-1/2 lbs	round steak, cut in 2-inch (5 cm) squares	1.5 kg
3	medium onions, sliced	3
3–4	tomatoes, sliced	3–4
6	Jerusalem artichokes, scraped and sliced	6

In a deep buttered 2-qt (2 L) casserole arrange layers of steak, onions and tomatoes, and top with a layer of artichoke slices. Add salt and pepper to taste and 1/2 cup (125 mL) water. Cover tightly and bake in preheated 350°F (180°C) oven for 90 minutes.
Serves 4 to 6

RED FLANNEL HASH

This is only one version of this popular New England dish.

1-1/2 lbs	round steak, ground	1.5 kg
1	can (16 oz/454 g) small beets, drained	1
1	can (15 oz/426 g) small new potatoes, drained	1
1-1/2 cups	milk	375 mL

Season round steak with salt and pepper and, in medium frying pan, sauté until it loses its red color. Chop the potatoes and beets. Combine all in shallow buttered 2-qt (2 L) casserole and bake in preheated 350°F (180°C) oven about 30 minutes.
Serves 4

MACARONI AND CHEESE BAKE

This dish has graced more tables than a Baptist preacher.

1 lb	elbow macaroni, cooked and drained	500 g
2	cans cream of chicken soup	2
4–5	tomatoes, sliced	4–5
12	slices process cheddar cheese	12

In medium bowl, place macaroni. In saucepan, heat soup with 3/4 cup (175 mL) water (or milk if you want a richer product). Mix soup with macaroni and place in buttered 9 × 12-inch (3.5 L) baking dish. Alternate slices of cheese and tomatoes over top (and optionally, sprinkle with chopped chives or oregano). Bake in preheated 350°F (180°C) oven for about 25 minutes.
Serves 10 to 12

LARA'S QUICK DINNER

Lara serves this with head lettuce wedges with Thousand Island dressing, and brown and serve rolls. Lara is 9 years old.

1	package (14 oz/398 g) macaroni and cheese dinner	1
1 lb	ground beef	500 g
1	jar (32 oz/910 g) spaghetti sauce with mushrooms	1

Cook macaroni and cheese dinner according to package directions. Meanwhile, in medium frying pan, cook beef until all pink color disappears. In medium saucepan, heat spaghetti sauce. Spoon finished macaroni and cheese dinner into bottom of serving dish. Cover with browned beef and pour hot spaghetti sauce over all.
Serves 6 to 8

TUNA-PEA CASSEROLE

Serve with baked potatoes and a salad.

1	can (7 oz/200 g) tuna, undrained	1
1	can (8 oz/227 g) green peas, drained	1
1/2 cup	chopped black olives	125 mL
1	can (10-1/2 oz/298 g) cream of mushroom soup	1

In a shallow 1-qt (1 L) baking dish, make a layer of the tuna and liquid, breaking the tuna into small pieces. Cover with the peas, then the olives, then the undiluted soup. Bake in preheated 300°F (140°C) oven for 30 minutes or until heated through.
Serves 4

TUNA-POTATO CHIP LOAF

Serve with green beans and rice pilaf.

1/2 cup	crushed potato chips	125 mL
1	can (7 oz/200 g) tuna, drained	1
1	can (10-1/2 oz/298 g) cream of mushroom soup	1
1/4 cup	chopped pimiento	50 mL

Mix all ingredients and bake in a greased 1-qt (1 L) loaf pan in preheated 350°F (180°C) oven for about 30 minutes, or until heated through.
Serves 4

GRANNY'S GOULASH

This proves the principle that plain things can taste good.

1 lb	lean ground beef	500 g
1	can (10-1/2 oz/298 g) chicken gumbo soup	1
1 Tbsp	mustard	15 mL
2 Tbsp	catsup	25 mL

In frying pan, brown ground beef. Add remaining ingredients, bring to a boil and simmer 5 minutes.
Serves 4

VEGETABLE GOULASH

This is an old Southern favourite.

4	tomatoes, chopped	4
2 cups	sliced okra	500 mL
1 cup	chopped onion	250 mL
1 cup	corn	250 mL

Combine all ingredients with salt and pepper to taste in a medium saucepan. Cover and bring to a boil. Cook about 15 minutes, remove cover, lower heat and simmer until thickened, about 15 minutes more.
Serves 4 to 6

Says Nancy C.: "After the pot roast I had in my crock pot had cooked for a few hours, I began to smell something really odd. I eventually discovered the recipe book between the heating unit and the top where the roast was cooking."

SOUR CREAM MACARONI

Surprisingly good.

1-1/2 cups	macaroni, cooked and drained	375 mL
4 Tbsp	melted butter	60 mL
1 cup	dairy sour cream	250 mL
1/2 cup	grated cheddar cheese	125 mL

In a greased 1-qt (1 L) casserole, toss macaroni with butter. Make a hollow in the center and pour in the sour cream. Sprinkle with cheese. Bake in preheated 400°F (200°C) oven until top is brown, about 30 minutes.
Serves 4

NOODLE-CHEESE RING

Serve a creamed meat, fish or vegetable mixture in the center. I like creamed peas and ham.

1	package (6 oz/170 g) egg noodles	1
3	eggs, beaten	3
1 cup	milk, scalded	250 mL
1-1/2 cups	grated cheddar cheese	375 mL

Break noodles into 1-inch (2.5 cm) pieces. Cook until barely tender in boiling, salted water; drain. Add eggs and milk; mix. Add cheese, 1 tsp (2 mL) salt and a pinch of pepper. Pour into greased ring mold, 8-1/2 inches (21 cm) in diameter. Bake in preheated 325°F (160°C) oven for 1 hour and 10 minutes, or until a knife inserted in the center comes out clean. Unmold and fill as desired.
Serves 4 to 6

SPAGHETTI PARMESAN

A basic, no frills recipe.

1/2 lb	spaghetti	250 g
1	clove garlic, minced	1
1/4 cup	olive oil	50 mL
1-1/2 cups	grated fresh Parmesan cheese	375 mL

Cook spaghetti according to package directions, adding garlic to water. Drain. Add remaining ingredients and toss lightly until well blended.
Serves 4

EASY NOODLES ALFREDO

Serve with a tossed salad and garlic bread.

1/2 lb	broad egg noodles	250 g
1/4 cup	sweet butter	50 mL
1/2 cup	grated fresh Parmesan cheese	125 mL
1 tsp	dried basil	2 mL

Cook noodles in large saucepan according to package directions; drain. Immediately return noodles to saucepan; place over low heat. Stir in butter. Continuing to stir, gradually add cheese and basil. Keep over low heat, stirring almost constantly, for 2 minutes to blend flavors.
Serves 4

TUNA SCALLOP

If you like tuna, you'll like this recipe.

1	package (7 oz/200 g) egg noodles	1
2 cups	tuna, drained and flaked	500 mL
1	can cream of mushroom soup	1
1 cup	grated cheddar cheese	1

Cook noodles according to package directions; drain. In 2-qt (2 L) greased baking dish, alternate layers of noodles, tuna, undiluted soup and cheese, ending with cheese. Bake in preheated 400°F (200°C) oven for about 20 minutes, or until brown on top.
Serves 4 to 6

SPAGHETTI WITH BUTTER SAUCE

If you want to be fancy you can call this "Spaghetti al Burro".

1 lb	spaghetti	500 g
1/4 lb	whipped sweet butter	125 g
1/2 cup	grated Parmesan cheese	125 mL
1 Tbsp	chopped fresh parsley	15 mL

Cook spaghetti according to package directions; drain. Toss spaghetti with half the butter. Season with salt and pepper. Sprinkle with grated cheese and parsley. Top with the rest of the butter, cut into little chips.
Serves 4 to 6

Tammy S. even managed to screw up a Kraft Dinner. "I put on the water to boil with some salt in it, then I added the noodles. When I saw the foam start to form I thought that I had soap in the pot so I threw out the noodles and went to the store for another package and tried again. When the same thing happened this time, I called my mother in tears. She's still laughing at me. . . ."

NOODLES ALSATIAN

An unusual dish.

3 Tbsp.	butter	45 mL
1/2 lb	egg noodles, cooked and drained	250 g
3 Tbsp	grated fresh Parmesan cheese	45 mL
1/4 cup	vegetable oil	50 mL

In saucepan, heat butter. Add about 2/3 of the noodles and season with salt and pepper. Cook over low heat for 5 minutes, stirring constantly. Add cheese and blend thoroughly. Turn into heated serving dish and keep hot. Chop remaining noodles very coarsely. In frying pan, heat vegetable oil. Add chopped noodles and cook until brown. Toss with noodles in dish. Serve hot.
Serves 4

SPÄTZLE

A Pennsylvania Dutch recipe.

3 cups	sifted all-purpose flour	750 mL
3	eggs, slightly beaten	3
1/4 cup	butter or margarine, melted	50 mL

In a medium bowl, combine flour, 1 tsp (2 mL) salt and 1/8 tsp (0.5 mL) white pepper. Make a well in the center. Add eggs and 1 cup water, and mix thoroughly. Scoop up dough on a spatula and cut off small pieces with a knife into boiling, salted water. As spätzle rises to the top, remove with slotted spoon and put in a covered bowl until all are cooked. Toss with butter and serve.
Serves 6

SPAGHETTI CARBONARA

This is a very inexpensive way to serve four people.

1 lb	spaghetti	500 g
1/2 lb	bacon	250 g
1	large clove garlic, halved	1
3	eggs, slightly beaten	3

Cook spaghetti according to package directions; drain. While spaghetti is cooking, cook bacon in large frying pan until crisp. Drain on paper toweling; crumble and reserve. Pour off all but 1/3 cup (75 mL) bacon fat. Sauté garlic in fat for 2 minutes; remove garlic. Return bacon to frying pan; heat just to warm bacon. Pour eggs over spaghetti; toss to mix well. Pour on bacon mixture and toss again.
Serves 4

Lorraine M. and Wendy G. are best friends, and both are newly-weds. One day they decided to make lasagna for their husbands. Lorraine takes up the story: "Around 7:00 P.M. we started the project. We brought several quarts of water to a rapid boil, added salt and a couple of drops of oil. We then read the instructions on the box of lasagna noodles, which said, 'Place one or two noodles at a time into boiling water, cook and drain.' We did JUST that. We boiled two noodles in that large pot of water until they were done. We took them out, and put in two more noodles. Also the water was boiling away and we had to stop and wait for fresh water to come to a rolling boil. This went on for hours. Finally we said to heck with it; what could happen if we did FOUR noodles at a time? Alongside these pots of boiling noodles were the contents of a pint-sized jar of sauce, bubbling away until there was only a crust around the edge of the pot. About 1:00 A.M. the whole shooting match went into the garbage, including the sauce pot."

NOODLES CARBONARA

A variation on the previous theme.

1 lb	egg noodles	500 g
1/2 lb	bacon	250 g
1/2 tsp	crushed red pepper	1 mL
1 cup	light cream	250 mL

Cook noodles according to package directions; drain. Cut bacon into 1-inch (2.5 cm) pieces. In large frying pan, cook bacon until crisp. Pour off drippings; return 4 Tbsp (60 mL) drippings to frying pan. Stir crushed red pepper into drippings and heat for a moment for flavors to blend. Add cream and heat to boiling. Toss with hot noodles until well coated. Sprinkle with grated Parmesan cheese if desired.
Serves 4 generously

Dee K. is the only one I know who has burned boiling water for spaghetti. She heard that if you add oil to the water then the noodles wouldn't stick. So she added a generous amount. The water boiled over, the oil caught on fire and she had a mess!

Fish And Seafood

"I was busy getting ready for a dinner party — you can imagine how my kitchen looked — and I whipped up a loaf of quick bread from scratch. When I put it on the counter to cool, it was immediately attacked by the 16-year-old bottomless pit I call a son. He quickly spit it out, however and asked what in the heck was in the loaf, because it tasted like FISH. Looking around, I realized that I had absent-mindedly dumped the bowl of leftover trout bits into the quick bread ingredients. . . .

BROILED SALMON STEAKS

This is good with broccoli and boiled potatoes.

3 Tbsp	white wine vinegar	45 mL
3 Tbsp	vegetable oil	45 mL
1 tsp	dried crumbled rosemary	5 mL
4	(about 2 lbs/1 kg) salmon steaks	4

In bowl, combine vinegar, oil and rosemary. Pour over salmon and marinate for at least 15 minutes at room temperature. Brush hot broiler pan with oil. Place salmon on broiler pan and broil about 3 inches (7.5 cm) from source of heat for about 10 minutes, or until fish flakes easily with a fork, turning fish halfway through cooking time. Season with salt and pepper.
Serves 4

WHITEFISH WITH CUCUMBERS

Go-alongs: little new potatoes and green peas.

1	cucumber, thinly sliced	1
4	whitefish fillets (about 2 lbs/1 kg)	4
2 tsp	lemon juice	10 mL
3 Tbsp	butter	45 mL

In the center of a large piece of foil, place overlapping slices of cucumber. Pat fish dry; arrange in a single layer on top of cucumber. Sprinkle with lemon juice and salt. Bring edges of foil together; fold to seal. Place on baking sheet. Bake in preheated 450°F (240°C) oven about 10 minutes, or until fish flakes easily with a fork. Serve with sauce made by creaming together 3 Tbsp (45 mL) butter with 2 tsp (10 mL) lemon juice (optional: add a little dried dill weed) and a pinch of salt.
Serves 4

CHEESY FISH STICKS

A new look for an old favorite.

2 lbs	fish sticks	1 kg
1	can (10-1/2 oz/298 g) cheddar cheese soup, undiluted	1
1 tsp	parsley flakes	5 mL
1 Tbsp	lemon juice	15 mL

In shallow baking dish, arrange fish sticks in a single layer. Mix remaining ingredients and pour over fish. Bake in preheated 350°F (180°C) oven for about 30 to 35 minutes. **Serves 4 to 6**

BAKED HADDOCK OR SOLE

An old Southern Florida recipe.

4	haddock or sole fillets (about 2 lbs/1 kg)	4
1	egg, lightly beaten	1
2/3 cup	cracker crumbs	150 mL
1/2 cup	butter	125 mL

Season fillets with salt and pepper. Dip in egg, then in cracker crumbs. Put butter into a shallow baking pan and place pan in preheated 400°F (200°C) oven until butter is melted and browned. Dip fillets in butter, coating them on both sides, and arrange in pan. Bake for 15 minutes, or until fish flakes easily with a fork, basting frequently with the butter. Remove pan from oven and continue basting until all butter is absorbed. **Serves 4**

ORANGE BROILED FILLETS

I first ate this in South Florida, where my hostess picked the
orange off a tree in her back yard.

4	whitefish fillets (about 2 lbs/1 kg)	4
1/4 cup	orange juice	50 mL
3 Tbsp	butter	45 mL
1 tsp	grated orange rind	5 mL

Place fillets in shallow baking pan. Mix orange juice with
melted butter and pour half this mixture over fish. Sprinkle
with salt, pepper and the orange rind. Bake for 10 minutes in
preheated 450°F (240°C) oven, then pour the rest of the
marinade over the fish and bake for about 10 minutes longer,
or until fish flakes easily with a fork.
Serves 4

SWORDFISH WITH ANCHOVY BUTTER

Feel free to add a little parsley on top before serving.

4	swordfish steaks (about 2 lbs/1 kg)	4
4 Tbsp	butter	60 mL
2 Tbsp	anchovy paste	25 mL
3 tsp	lemon juice	15 mL

Place steaks in broiler pan and brush with butter on both
sides. Place under broiler, about 3 inches (7.5 cm) from source
of heat, and broil for 5 to 8 minutes on each side, or until fish
flakes easily with a fork. Mix the rest of the butter (you may
need more than 4 Tbsp/60 mL) with the anchovy paste and
lemon juice and pour on top of the hot steaks.
Serves 4

PAN BROILED HALIBUT STEAKS

Make this just for the halibut!

3 Tbsp	olive or vegetable oil	45 mL
4	halibut steaks, about 3/4-inch (2 cm) thick	4
1/2 tsp	dried basil	2 mL
2 Tbsp	lemon juice	25 mL

In a large, wide frying pan, heat oil over medium heat. Add steaks and sprinkle with basil. Cook for about 3 to 5 minutes per side, or until fish flakes easily with a fork. Sprinkle with lemon juice, salt and pepper. This entrée has only about 200 calories per serving.
Serves 4

BROILED TROUT

I like this served with kasha and an endive and orange salad.

4	(10 oz/284 g each) trout	4
4 Tbsp	French dressing	60 mL
2 Tbsp	instant minced onion	25 mL
	Thin lemon slices (optional)	

Dress trout for cooking. Rinse under cold running water and dry thoroughly. Brush cavities of fish with French dressing and sprinkle generously with salt and instant minced onion. Brush outsides of trout generously with French dressing and arrange on a greased large shallow baking pan on a broiler rack. Broil about 3 inches (7.5 cm) from source of heat for 5 to 8 minutes on each side, or until fish flakes easily with a fork. Brush with dressing during broiling. Remove to heated platter and garnish with lemon slices if desired.
Serves 4

BAKED RED SNAPPER

The first time I made this I had caught the snapper (all 8 lbs/ 4 kg of him!) off the coast of St. Petersburg, Florida.

4	red snapper fillets (about 1/2 lb/250 g each)	4
4 Tbsp	butter	60 mL
	Thin lemon or lime slices	

Line a shallow baking dish with aluminum foil. Lay the fillets, skin side down, on the foil. Spread 1 Tbsp (25 mL) of butter over each fillet. Garnish fish with lemon or lime slices. Bake, uncovered, in preheated 350°F (180°C) oven about 30 minutes, or until fillets flake easily with a fork. Baste with extra butter if fish becomes too dry. Serve with tartar sauce, if desired.
Serves 4

PIKE'S PEAK

Cooked outdoors over an open fire, nothing can beat this.

2 lbs	sliced filleted pike	1 kg
2	eggs, well beaten	2
1 cup	yellow cornmeal	250 mL
1 qt	fat for deep frying	1 L

Cut fillets into small slices. Sprinkle slices with salt and pepper; dip into egg and then into cornmeal, coating well. Fry in deep hot fat for 3 to 4 minutes, or until fish is golden brown on all sides. Drain on paper toweling and serve immediately.
Serves 4 to 6

"Please send me a Kitchen Klutz certificate for Lana E.," writes John A. "Her idea of surf and turf is fish and steak cooked together in the same pan!"

CRABMEAT FISH SQUARES

A way to dress up everyday fish squares.

6	breaded fish squares	6
1	can cream of chicken soup	1
1	egg yolk, lightly beaten	1
1	can (6 oz/170 g) crabmeat	1

Cook fish squares according to package directions. While they are baking, put cream of chicken soup in small saucepan and heat. Beat in egg yolk; then blend in crabmeat. Add salt and pepper to taste. Serve hot over fish squares.
Serves 6

ANGELA'S BAKED SNAPPER

Good with rice cooked in clam juice, a tossed salad and bread sticks.

3 Tbsp	olive oil	45 mL
1	whole red snapper (about 3 lbs/1.5 kg) cleaned and gutted	1
4	sprigs fresh basil or thyme	4
1/2	lemon, sliced	1/2

Line a large shallow baking pan with aluminum foil. Brush foil lightly with oil. Measure thickness of fish. Put fish on baking sheet and brush both sides with remaining oil. Put lemon slices and herbs inside fish cavity. Bake in preheated 425°F (220°C) oven for 10 minutes for each inch (2.5 cm) of thickness (for example, 30 minutes for 3 inches/7.5 cm). Test by flaking with a fork at the thickest part of the fish.
Serves 4

SCALLOPED OYSTERS

This dish has been made this way since the earliest days of the settlers.

1 pint	oysters, drained	500 mL
1 cup	strained oyster liquid and table cream	250 mL
1-1/2 cups	cracker crumbs	375 mL
4 Tbsp	melted butter	60 mL

Pick over oysters to make sure there is no shell in them. In a buttered casserole, place a layer of oysters. Top with a layer of crumbs and salt and pepper to taste. Repeat layer. Pour oyster liquid and cream over all. Then pour butter over all. Bake in preheated 400°F (200°C) oven for 20 minutes.
Serves 4

HAM AND OYSTERS

I begged this recipe from the chef at a restaurant in Williamsburg, Virginia.

1 qt	oysters	1 L
4	large thin slices country ham, cooked	4
4	sprigs parsley or watercress	4
1	lemon, quartered	1

Pick over oysters to make sure there is no shell in them. In a frying pan, cook oysters in their own juice over low heat for about 2 minutes. Sprinkle freshly ground black pepper over them. Cover oysters with ham slices. Continue cooking gently until the edges of the oysters curl and they are plump. Remove from heat. Place one slice of ham on each plate and pile oysters on top of the ham. Garnish with parsley or watercress, and lemon wedge.
Serves 4

SHRIMP SHARON

Developed by my friend, Sharon, for a ladies' luncheon.

1 lb	cooked shrimp	500 g
1/4 cup	butter	50 mL
3 tsp	chopped fresh dill	15 mL
1/2 cup	dry white wine	125 mL

In buttered casserole dish, place shrimp. Dot with butter and sprinkle with dill, 1 tsp (5 mL) salt and 1/4 tsp (1 mL) freshly ground black pepper. Pour the wine over all and heat in a preheated 350°F (180°C) oven for about 10 minutes, basting once or twice with the butter. Garnish with sprigs of watercress or parsley if desired.
Serves 4

"One of my father's favorite foods," writes Martha F., "is deep fried clams. One day he attempted to make them at home. He bought an electric fryer for deep frying, several bottles of corn oil, and three pounds of clams. He made a cornmeal batter and heated the oil to the proper temperature. He lowered the cooking basket of ice-cold clams into the bubbling oil and it erupted like Mt. Vesuvius, shooting hot oil into the air, covering the counter tops and running in streams down the grout onto the ceramic tile floor. His reaction? He cleaned it up (sort of) and tried it again. Same thing happened (maybe worse). So he sent my brother out for more oil. By this time my mother had left the house, afraid she'd say something she'd regret. Dad repeated the scenario three times. We never did get to eat any clams."

FRIED BUTTERFLY SHRIMP

Great with french fries and a tossed salad.

2 lbs	raw shrimp in shells	1 kg
1/2 cup	buttermilk	150 mL
1 cup	all-purpose flour	250 mL
1 qt	fat for deep frying	1 L

Shell shrimp and remove black vein. Wash shrimp and cut through back on outside; then spread out. Dip in buttermilk, then in flour to which salt and pepper have been added. Deep fry in hot fat until lightly browned. Drain on paper toweling and serve at once.
Serves 4

SCALLOP SAUTÉ

A very simple but very luscious recipe.

1 lb	scallops	500 g
1/4 cup	all-purpose flour	50 mL
1/4 cup	butter	50 mL
Pinch	dried dillweed	Pinch

Wipe scallops with damp paper toweling. Roll in flour seasoned with salt and pepper. In frying pan, melt butter. Add scallops and cook over high heat for no longer than 5 or 6 minutes, tossing constantly so they will cook evenly. Sprinkle with dillweed. Serve immediately.
Serves 4

SCALLOPS À LA MARINARA

If you want to make your own marinara sauce, see Page 134.

4 Tbsp	butter	60 mL
4 Tbsp	dry white wine	60 mL
2 lbs	scallops	1 kg
1/4 cup	marinara sauce	50 mL

In frying pan, melt butter. Add wine. When mixture is hot, put in the scallops and season with salt and pepper. Cook over low heat, turning frequently, until almost done, about 4 minutes. Drain the scallops, return them to the frying pan, and add the marinara sauce. Stir and cook for about 3 minutes more. Serve at once.
Serves 4

BOILED LOBSTER

Be sure the lobsters are alive when you put them in the pot.

4	live lobsters (about 2-1/2 lbs/1.5 kg each)	4
	Melted butter	
	Lemon wedges	

In a big pot, put the lobsters with sea water or salted cold water to cover well. Bring the water to a boil and cook for five minutes. Reduce heat and simmer for about 15 minutes. Drain and serve at once, leaving the head, body and tail intact. Serve with melted butter and lemon wedges.
Serves 4

BROILED LOBSTER TAILS

If using frozen lobster tails, thaw before cooking.

4	lobster tails	4
1/4 cup	butter	50 mL
1/4 cup	olive oil	50 mL
4 tsp	lemon juice	20 mL

Split the lobster tails through the membrane, but do not remove the meat from the shells. Marinate for several hours in the refrigerator in a mixture of the butter, olive oil and lemon juice. Broil, about 3 inches (7.5 cm) from source of heat, for 10 to 15 minutes, depending on size, basting frequently with the marinade. Serve hot with the drippings, or extra butter and lemon slices.
Serves 4

BROILED KING CRAB LEGS

You will find the giant Alaskan king crab legs in the frozen food section of your supermarket.

4	king crab legs	4
1/4 cup	melted butter	50 mL
4 tsp	lemon juice	20 mL

Break the crab legs into sections, slit the roundest side of the shells lengthwise with scissors, snip them crosswise in several places along the slit, and pull it open about an inch (2.5 cm). Place on broiler pan and brush with a mixture of the butter and lemon juice. Grind pepper over them and broil, about 5 inches (12.5 cm) from source of heat, just until the shells begin to brown, basting several times with the sauce.
Serves 4 generously

"I just about lost my husband," writes Joyce A. "As a bride, I was happy to make my hard rock miner's lunches for work. He liked salmon with a touch of vinegar (yuk). But this time I forgot to put his cigarettes and matches in the pail. When he returned home I was very apologetic about forgetting them, and he replied, 'It's a good thing you did or I might have blown up!' Instead of mixing the salmon with vinegar, I had grabbed the wrong bottle — I had added Varsol! Needless to say we have been married 21 happy years and I've never had to make another lunch."

BROILED SOFT SHELL CRABS

These also may be sautéed over medium heat in a little butter or shortening.

8	soft shell crabs	8
1/2 cup	melted butter	125 mL
3 Tbsp	lemon juice	45 mL
Pinch	cayenne pepper	Pinch

Wash crabs and dry with paper toweling. Dip in a mixture of the melted butter, lemon juice, cayenne pepper and a pinch of black pepper, then roll in flour. Place crabs on broiling pan and broil about 2 inches (5 cm) from source of heat, for about 10 minutes, turning once. Serve with extra melted butter and lemon juice.
Serves 4

Vegetables

Carol F. speaks of microwaves: "I was cooking a whole spaghetti squash, but I guess I didn't pierce the skin deeply enough. The boom that came from the oven told the whole story and it was some time before I worked up enough courage to open the door. When I did, the part that had hit the door slid off and formed a gooey pile at my feet, while the remainder clung tenaciously to the walls and roof, causing the oven to take on the appearance of the Carlsbad Caverns."

ASPARAGUS WITH LEMON BUTTER

A tried and true favorite.

2-1/2 lbs	fresh asparagus, washed and trimmed	1.5 kg
2 Tbsp	fresh lemon juice	25 mL
1/4 lb	(8 Tbsp/120 mL) butter	125 g
	Lemon wedges	

In saucepan, cook asparagus in boiling salted water just until tender, about 12 minutes. Combine lemon juice and 2 Tbsp (25 mL) of the butter in small saucepan; heat until bubbly. Gradually add remaining butter, stirring until blended. Drain asparagus. Arrange on platter. Spoon lemon butter over asparagus. Garnish with lemon wedges.
Serves 4 to 6

ASPARAGUS PARMESAN

Great with steak and french fries.

1-1/2 lbs	fresh asparagus	750 g
4 Tbsp	butter, melted	60 mL
1/4 cup	dry white wine	50 mL
1/2 cup	freshly grated Parmesan cheese	125 mL

Wash and trim asparagus. In saucepan, cook asparagus in boiling salted water until tender-crisp, about 10 minutes; drain well. Place asparagus in shallow baking dish. Pour melted butter and wine over it. Sprinkle with freshly grated black pepper. Coat the top heavily with Parmesan cheese. Bake in preheated 400°F (200°C) oven for 10 to 15 minutes, or until cheese melts. Serve hot.
Serves 4

GINGER BEANS

Kudos to whoever thought this one up!

2	cans (1 lb/500 g each) pork and beans in tomato sauce	2
1/2 cup	finely crushed gingersnaps	125 mL
1/4 cup	catsup	50 mL
2 Tbsp	light molasses	25 mL

In 1-qt (1 L) casserole, combine beans, gingersnaps, catsup, molasses and 1/2 tsp (2 mL) salt. Cover and bake in preheated 350°F (180°C) oven for 30 minutes. You could cut a can of luncheon meat into six slices and bake it on top, for a main dish.
Serves 4 to 6

BARBECUE BEANS

Those who like them sweet will adore these.

1/2 cup	chopped celery	125 mL
7 cups	pork and beans in tomato sauce	1.75 L
2	cans (4 oz/115 g each) Vienna sausages, drained	2
1 cup	brown sugar	250 mL

Place celery in bottom of a 2-1/2-qt (2.5 L) casserole. Pour in 3-1/2 cups (875 mL) of beans. Arrange sausages on top and cover with 3-1/2 cups (875 mL) of beans. Sprinkle with brown sugar. Cover and bake in preheated 300°F (140°C) oven for 2 hours.
Serves 8

PENNSYLVANIA DUTCH LIMA BEANS

A Mennonite housewife fixed these for me in Lancaster, Pennsylvania.

1 lb	fresh lima beans	500 g
4	large potatoes, peeled and diced	4
2 cups	milk	500 mL
2 Tbsp	butter	25 mL

In covered saucepan, partially cook lima beans in boiling salted water. Add potatoes and continue cooking until vegetables are tender; drain. Add milk, butter, salt and pepper to taste; stir gently. Heat through.
Serves about 8

JEAN'S SPECIAL LIMAS

This is from my good friend, Jean Vincent of Flint, Michigan.

2	packages (10 oz/284 g each) frozen baby lima beans	2
1	can (4 oz/115 g) pimientos, chopped	1
1/4 cup	butter	50 mL

Cook lima beans according to package directions; drain. Mix cooked beans with drained pimientos and salt and pepper to taste. Here you can add 1/4 tsp (1 mL) celery seed if you have it. Add butter and toss well so butter melts.
Serves 6

HARVARD BEETS

I wonder if these were ever actually served at Harvard?

1	can (1 lb/500 g) sliced or diced beets	1
1 Tbsp	cornstarch	15 mL
1/2 cup	sugar	125 mL
1/2 cup	cider vinegar	125 mL

Drain beets; reserve 1/2 cup (125 mL) liquid. In saucepan, combine cornstarch and sugar. Gradually stir in vinegar, reserved liquid, and 3/4 tsp (3 mL) salt. Cook over medium heat, stirring constantly, until thick and clear. Add beets, heat to serving temperature.
Serves 4

BEETS À LA PARÉE

Tart and tasty.

4 cups	diced cooked beets	1 L
3 Tbsp	tart French dressing	45 mL
1	small onion, minced	1

In saucepan, combine all ingredients, 3/4 tsp (3 mL) salt and 1/8 tsp (0.5 mL) pepper and heat thoroughly.
Serves 6

BROCCOLI ALMONDINE

Everyone's favorite.

2	packages (10 oz/284 g each) frozen broccoli spears	2
1/4 cup	butter	50 mL
1/2 cup	slivered almonds	125 mL
2 Tbsp	lemon juice	25 mL

Cook broccoli according to package directions. Drain and place in serving dish. Meanwhile, in small frying pan, melt butter. Add almonds and cook gently several minutes until they are crisp and golden. Add lemon juice and stir. Pour sauce over broccoli.
Serves about 6

BROCCOLI WITH LEMON BUTTER

Harried cook's favorite; it's so easy.

1	medium bunch broccoli	1
3 Tbsp	butter	45 mL
2 Tbsp	lemon juice	25 mL

Wash and trim broccoli and cut into florets. In saucepan, cook broccoli in boiling, salted water to cover just until tender; drain. In small frying pan or saucepan, melt butter. Add lemon juice and salt and pepper to taste. Heat gently. Place broccoli in serving bowl and pour sauce over it.
Serves 4

BEEFY BRUSSELS SPROUTS

Start these the day before.

2	packages (10 oz/284 g each) frozen Brussels sprouts, cooked and drained	2
1	beef bouillon cube	1
3 Tbsp	butter or margarine	45 mL
1/2 cup	freshly grated Parmesan cheese	125 mL

Place sprouts in 1-qt (1 L) casserole. Heat together 1 cup (250 mL) water, the beef bouillon cube, and butter. Pour over Brussels sprouts and refrigerate overnight. When ready to bake, sprinkle with Parmesan cheese and bake in preheated 325°F (160°C) oven for 30 minutes, or until heated through.
Serves 6

GLAZED BRUSSELS SPROUTS

I first ate these on the Chesapeake Bay in Virginia.

2 lbs	fresh Brussels sprouts, trimmed	1 kg
1	small onion, sliced	1
1 tsp	caraway seeds	5 mL
4 Tbsp	butter	60 mL

In bowl or saucepan, soak sprouts in lukewarm water for 20 minutes. Drain. Drop them into a saucepan containing enough boiling salted water to cover them. Add onion and caraway seeds to water. Cook for 10 to 15 minutes, or until sprouts are tender; drain well. In frying pan, melt butter. Sauté sprouts over low heat, shaking the pan often, until sprouts are glazed and golden, but not brown.
Serves 6

CABBAGE WITH NOODLES

Add 1/2 tsp (2 mL) caraway seed to cooking cabbage if desired.

1	medium head cabbage, quartered	1
1/2 lb	egg noodles	250 g
3	medium onions, sliced	3
4 Tbsp	butter or margarine	60 mL

Quarter cabbage and cut away the thicker part of the core.
Bring a large saucepan of water to a boil and drop in the cabbage quarters; cook until tender; drain. In another saucepan
of boiling salted water, cook the noodles just until tender;
drain well and mix in 2 Tbsp (25 mL) butter. In frying pan,
sauté the onions in the remaining butter until transparent.
Chop cabbage, return to saucepan, and add onions. Stir over
low heat for 10 minutes. Mix in buttered noodles. Add salt
and pepper to taste and serve immediately.
Serve 6 to 8

CABBAGE MEDLEY

Start with a convenience food.

2	packages (10 oz/284 g each) frozen cabbage in butter sauce, cooked according to package directions	2
1	can (10-1/2 oz/298 g) cream of celery soup	1
8	strips bacon, fried crisp and diced	8
1/4 cup	packaged bread crumbs	50 mL

In a 1-1/2-qt (1.5 L) casserole, blend hot cooked cabbage and
butter sauce, soup and bacon. Sprinkle crumbs over top. Bake
in preheated 400°F (200°C) oven for 15 minutes.
Serves 4 to 6

CARROT COINS

Coin of the carrot realm.

3-1/2 cups	carrots, peeled and cut into thin slices	875 mL
2 Tbsp	unsalted butter	25 mL
1 Tbsp	apricot jam	25 mL
1 Tbsp	maple syrup	25 mL

In saucepan, cook carrots in boiling salted water just until tender. Drain, return to saucepan and toss with butter, jam and maple syrup until well coated. Season lightly with salt and pepper.
Serves 4 to 6

CARROTS IN MARMALADE

Another good way to cook mature carrots.

4 cups	peeled carrots, thinly sliced	1 L
1/3 cup	orange juice	75 mL
1/4 tsp	ginger	1 mL
1/3 cup	orange marmalade	75 mL

In bowl, combine carrots, orange juice, 1/2 tsp (2 mL) salt, ginger and marmalade. Turn into a buttered 1-1/2-qt (1.5 L) casserole. Dot with butter if desired. Bake, covered, in preheated 350°F (180°C) oven for 30 minutes or until carrots are tender. Sprinkle with snipped parsley if desired.
Serves 6 to 8

PINEAPPLE POACHED CARROTS

Double the recipe for six persons.

2 cups	carrots, peeled and cut in julienne strips	500 mL
3/4 cup	(6 oz/170 g) pineapple juice	375 mL
3/4 tsp	cinnamon	4 mL
1/8 tsp	nutmeg (optional)	0.5 mL

In medium saucepan, combine all ingredients and freshly ground pepper to taste. Bring to a boil, reduce heat, cover pan, and simmer for about 10 minutes, or until carrots are tender-crisp.

Serves 3

HONEY-GLAZED CARROTS

The perfect go-along for ham.

1 lb	carrots, peeled	500 g
3 Tbsp	butter	45 mL
1-1/2 tsp	liquid honey	7 mL
1 tsp	lemon juice	5 mL

Using vegetable peeler or food processor, shred carrots into long strands. Place in saucepan, cover with boiling, salted water and cook for 2 minutes, or just until barely tender. Drain and rinse under cold running water; drain again. In frying pan, melt butter over medium heat. Stir in honey and lemon juice. Mix well. Add carrots; stir and toss for 2 to 3 minutes, or until carrots are heated through and well coated. Season with freshly ground black pepper, and nutmeg if desired.

Serves 4

CREAMY BAKED CAULIFLOWER

Delicious with baked ham.

1	large head cauliflower	1
1-1/2 cups	heavy cream	375 mL
1 cup	grated Gruyere cheese	250 mL

Trim green leaves from cauliflower and cut into florets. Cut tender parts of stems into bite-sized pieces. In saucepan, cook cauliflower in boiling salted water for 5 minutes; drain. Place cauliflower in ovenproof dish. Season cream with salt and pepper and pour over the cauliflower. Cover with grated cheese and bake in preheated 450°F (240°C) oven for 20 minutes.
Serves 6 to 8

CAULIFLOWER WITH BUTTER AND LEMON

An elementary recipe.

1	medium head cauliflower	1
1/4 cup	melted butter	50 mL
	Juice of 1/2 lemon	

Trim green leaves from cauliflower. Cut off stem even with cauliflower. In saucepan, boil cauliflower in boiling salted water until tender, about 15 to 20 minutes. Drain and place in serving bowl. Pour melted butter and lemon juice over cauliflower. Add salt and pepper to taste.
Serves 4 to 6

Robert LaR. says that since his wife works, he feels that it's only fair to start dinner when he gets home earlier than she. "One evening I took the bowl of vegetables from the fridge and dumped them into the pressure cooker. I then added the meat, plus the necessary seasonings and water. Presto! Dinner was underway. When my wife got home I proudly opened the cooker and started to serve dinner. It was then that I discovered a well cooked "J Cloth" nestled in the meat and veggies. . ."

KIDS' FAVORITE GRILLED CORN

You should see them gobble these up.

8	ears fresh corn	8
1/2 cup	creamy peanut butter	125 mL
8	slices bacon	8

Turn back husks of corn and remove silk. Spread each ear of corn with 1 Tbsp (15 mL) of peanut butter. Spiral a slice of bacon, barber-pole style, around each ear. Lay husks back into position. Place on grill over hot coals; turn frequently until done, about 20 minutes.
Serves 8

GOURMET CORN

Contributed by my niece, Debby Hawley.

1	package (3 oz/85 g) cream cheese	1
1/4 cup	light cream	50 mL
2 Tbsp	butter	25 mL
2 cups	whole kernel corn, drained	500 mL

In a frying pan, combine softened cream cheese, cream, butter, and 1/2 tsp (2 mL) salt (onion salt is best). Stir mixture over low heat until cheese melts. Add corn; heat through, and serve.
Serves 4

BRAISED CUCUMBERS

They're not exclusively for salads.

3	medium cucumbers	3
2 Tbsp	butter	25 mL
1	beef bouillon cube	1

Peel cucumbers; cut crosswise in half, then quarter lengthwise.
In frying pan, heat butter. Brown cucumbers lightly. Add
bouillon cube dissolved in 1 Tbsp (15 mL) boiling water. Cook,
covered, over low heat for about 5 minutes, or just until tender.
Add salt and pepper to taste.
Serves 4

CUCUMBERS WITH DILL

A subtle flavor.

2	cucumbers	2
2 Tbsp	butter	25 mL
1	red onion, thinly sliced	1
3 Tbsp	coarsely chopped fresh dill	45 mL

Peel cucumbers; cut in half lengthwise and remove seeds.
Sprinkle with salt and let stand for 20 minutes on paper toweling; pat dry. Cut into 1/4-inch (0.5 cm) slices; set aside. In large
frying pan, melt butter over medium high heat. Add onion and
cook, stirring constantly, until translucent, about 1 minute.
Stir in cucumbers and sprinkle lightly with pepper; cook, stirring occasionally, for 2 to 3 minutes, or until cucumbers are
cooked through but still crunchy. Sprinkle with dill and toss.
Taste and adjust seasoning if necessary. Serve immediately.
Serves 4

EGGPLANT WITH PECANS

I like almost anything with pecans in it.

1	medium eggplant (about 1-1/2 lbs/750 g)	1
1/3 cup	butter	75 mL
1 cup	milk	250 mL
1/3 cup	chopped pecans	75 mL

Wash eggplant and without peeling cut it into 1/4-inch (0.5 cm) thick slices. In frying pan, melt butter. Sauté eggplant slices until lightly brown on both sides. Place in shallow baking dish, cover with milk and sprinkle with nuts and salt and pepper to taste. Bake in preheated 300°F (140°C) oven for about 1 hour.
Serves 4

EGGPLANT PARMIGIANA

Mama mia!

1	large eggplant (about 2 lbs/1 kg)	1
1/4 cup	vegetable oil	125 mL
1-1/2 cups	canned tomato sauce	375 mL
1/2 lb	thinly sliced mozzarella cheese	250 g

Peel and slice eggplant 1/2-inch (1 cm) thick. In frying pan, heat a small amount of oil and sauté eggplant slices. Drain on paper toweling. In shallow baking dish, arrange layers of eggplant, tomato sauce, and sliced cheese, ending with tomato sauce and cheese. Bake in preheated 375°F (190°C) oven about 25 minutes, or until well browned.
Serves 4 or 5

CREAMED CURRY ONIONS

An exotic flavor.

1	can (1 lb/500 g) canned small onions	1
1	can (10-1/2 oz/298 g) cream of mushroom soup	1
1/3 cup	milk or light cream	75 mL
1/4 tsp	curry powder	1 mL

Drain onions. In saucepan, blend soup, milk and curry powder; add onions. Heat slowly, stirring once or twice, until bubbly and hot.
Serves about 4

BETTE'S ONION DISH

Bette got me hooked on these.

4	large cooking onions	4
1/4 cup	honey	50 mL
1 tsp	soy sauce	5 mL
1 tsp	prepared mustard	5 mL

Cut off tops and bottoms of onions; remove outer skin. Place onions in saucepan and add enough water to come to a depth of 1 inch (2.5 cm); cover and bring to a boil. Reduce heat to medium and cook for 30 minutes, or until tender. Drain and transfer onions to small greased casserole. In small saucepan, combine honey, soy sauce and mustard. Cook over medium heat, stirring, for 5 minutes. Pour over onions and bake, uncovered, in preheated 350°F (180°C) oven for 30 to 40 minutes, or until heated through and glazed. Cut each onion in half to serve.
Serves 8

ZEKE'S LEEKS

A leek is a green onion with a college education.

2	bunches (8 to 10) leeks	2
4 Tbsp	butter or margarine	60 mL
1/2 tsp	celery salt	2 mL

Trim roots and about three-quarters of the green tops from leeks; split each leek lengthwise; wash well. Arrange pieces, cut side down, in a large frying pan. Add just enough water to cover; heat to boiling, cover. Simmer 5 minutes; drain; return to pan. Add butter; sprinkle with salt and celery salt. Cook slowly 5 minutes longer, or until leeks are tender.
Serves 6

LEEKS IN SOUR CREAM

What would we do without sour cream?

8	medium leeks	8
1/2 cup	dairy sour cream	125 mL
1/2 tsp	dry mustard	2 mL
1/4 cup	freshly grated cheese	50 mL

Trim roots and about three-quarters of the green tops from leeks; split each leek lengthwise; wash well. In frying pan, simmer prepared leeks in salted water just until tender, about 5 minutes; drain thoroughly. Arrange close together in a shallow greased baking dish; pour in sour cream mixed with mustard; sprinkle with cheese. Place under broiler until bubbly.
Serves 4

BENJIE'S MUSHROOMS

Good served on hot buttered toast.

1 lb	fresh mushrooms, cleaned	500 g
2 Tbsp	butter	25 mL
1/4 cup	table cream	50 mL
2	egg yolks, beaten	2

In saucepan, cook mushrooms and butter in a very small amount of water for a few minutes. Season with salt and pepper to taste. Add cream. Remove from heat and stir in egg yolks. Return to heat for a few minutes to thicken egg yolks, and serve at once.
Serves 4

BAKED MUSHROOMS

You'll love these!

1 lb	fresh mushrooms, cleaned and sliced	500 g
2 cups	small soft French bread cubes	500 mL
1/3 cup	butter, melted	75 mL
1/3 cup	chicken stock or broth	75 mL

Butter a 1-1/2-qt (1.5 L) casserole and add about one-third of the mushrooms. Sprinkle them with one-third of the bread cubes; drizzle with one-third of the melted butter. Sprinkle lightly with salt and pepper. Repeat layers once; set remaining bread cubes and butter aside. Top casserole with remainder of mushrooms and a sprinkling of salt and pepper. Pour chicken stock or broth over all. Cover and bake in preheated 350°F (180°C) oven for 20 minutes. Combine remaining bread cubes and butter and sprinkle over top of the mushroom mixture. Bake an additional 10 minutes, uncovered.
Serves 6

SNOW PEAS WITH PEPPERS

This has only about 65 calories per serving.

1/2 lb	snow peas	250 g
1	sweet red pepper, cored and seeded	1
2 Tbsp	butter	25 mL
4	green onions, thinly sliced	4

Trim and wash snow peas. Cut red pepper into julienne strips.
Set aside. In large frying pan, heat butter over medium heat.
Add green onions and sauté for about 1 minute, or until soft.
Add red pepper and sauté for 2 minutes. Add snow peas and
sauté 2 minutes. Sprinkle with salt and pepper and serve
immediately.
Serves 4

SNOW PEAS WITH MUSHROOMS

Elegant!

1 lb	snow peas	500 g
1 lb	fresh mushrooms	500 g
1/4 cup	butter	50 mL
2 Tbsp	chopped parsley	25 mL

Trim snow peas, wash and drain. In saucepan, cook snow peas
in small amount of boiling salted water just until heated
through. Drain at once; reserve. In frying pan, sauté mushrooms quickly in butter. Toss with snow peas. Season to taste
with salt and pepper and sprinkle with chopped parsley.
Serves 6

PEAS WITH ONIONS

Bake it while the rest of the meal is being prepared.

1 tsp	dried mint	5 mL
1	package (10 oz/284 g) frozen peas	1
8	small cooked onions	8
3 Tbsp	butter	45 mL

In small casserole, combine mint and 2 Tbsp (25 mL) water.
Add peas, onions, butter and salt and pepper to taste. Cover
and bake in preheated 375°F (190°C) oven for 50 minutes.
Serves 4

PEAS WITH MUSHROOMS

A favorite around our house.

1-1/2 cups	cooked mushrooms	375 mL
1 Tbsp	chopped onion	15 mL
2 Tbsp	butter or margarine	25 mL
2 cups	frozen peas, cooked and drained	500 mL

In heavy saucepan, sauté mushrooms and onion in butter until
onion is golden. Add peas and a dash of pepper; heat through.
Serves 4 to 6

POTATO PIE

This is a very economical, meatless main dish.

1	box (6 oz/170 g) hash browned potatoes with onions	1
4	eggs	4
2 cups	cottage cheese	500 mL
2 Tbsp	chopped parsley	25 mL

Rehydrate hash browns according to package directions; drain thoroughly. In medium bowl, slightly beat eggs; add potatoes, cottage cheese, parsley and 1/4 tsp (1 mL) pepper; mix well. Turn into well greased 9-inch (23 cm) pie plate; smooth top. Bake in preheated 350°F (180°C) oven 35 to 40 minutes, or until set and lightly browned. Let stand 10 minutes before cutting.
Serves 4

POTATO PUFF

Delicious with steak.

2 cups	mashed potatoes	500 mL
2	eggs, separated	2
1 cup	milk	250 mL
2 Tbsp	butter	25 mL

In bowl, beat egg yolks until very light. Have mashed potatoes in a bowl. To potatoes, add beaten egg yolks, milk, butter and 1/4 tsp (1 mL) pepper. In another bowl, beat egg whites until stiff. Fold beaten egg whites into mashed potato mixture. Place in well greased 1-1/2-qt (1.5 L) casserole. Set in a pan containing hot water and bake in preheated 325°F (160°C) oven for 1-1/2 hours.
Serves 4 to 6

EASY SCALLOPED POTATOES

Just remember: one of everything.

1	package (16 oz/454 g) frozen crinkle-cut cottage fried potatoes	1
1	medium onion, chopped	1
1	can (13 oz/370 g) evaporated milk	1

In a 1-1/2 to 2-qt (1.5 to 2 L) casserole, mix ingredients and 1 tsp (5 mL) salt. Bake in preheated 375°F (190°C) oven, stirring occasionally, 40 to 45 minutes, or until potatoes are tender and milk is absorbed.
Serves 4

VINNIE'S SCALLOPED POTATOES

Vinnie was our neighbor's cook for many years.

5	large potatoes, sliced thin	5
2	large onions, sliced thin	2
2 cups	milk	500 mL
4 Tbsp	butter	60 mL

Peel and thinly slice potatoes and onions. Into a 9 × 13-inch (22.5 × 32.5 cm) baking dish, put a layer of potatoes, salt and pepper to taste, and dots of butter. Add a layer of onions, sprinkled with salt and pepper and dotted with butter. Repeat until all potatoes and onions are used. Pour enough milk over to cover potatoes and onions. Bake in 350°F (180°C) oven until potatoes are well browned, about 1 hour. Cook immediately upon preparing them so potatoes won't darken.
Serves 6

RICE WITH TOMATO SAUCE AND CHEESE

Be sure to use freshly grated cheese.

6 Tbsp	butter	90 mL
6 cups	cooked white rice	1.5 L
2 cups	canned tomato sauce	500 mL
1-1/4 cups	freshly grated Parmesan cheese	300 mL

In a frying pan, melt the butter. Add rice and cook, stirring, until heated through and lightly browned. Place rice in warmed serving bowl. Heat the tomato sauce and pour over rice; sprinkle with cheese. Lift and toss the rice to coat kernels.
Serves 6 to 8

LEMON-DILL RICE

Great with fish.

3 cups	hot cooked rice	750 mL
1/4 cup	chopped fresh dill	50 mL
2 tsp	grated lemon peel	10 mL

Into hot cooked rice, stir dill and lemon peel.
Serves 4 to 6

Of his beautiful wife, Barb, Rick T. says: "Although Barb is an excellent cook, her moments in the kitchen are far too many to mention. Her reputation has spread far and wide, from Vancouver to Halifax. Among our friends and relations she has given rise to a new verb — "to Barb out." Barbing out or just Barbing covers all incidences of clumsiness or accidents causing minor injury, any degree of embarassment, or mess in the kitchen. Although I love her dearly and she is the best thing that ever happened to me, I must say that she is the proverbial accident looking for a place to happen. . . ."

GREEN RICE

It looks pretty on the plate.

2/3 cup	regular rice	150 mL
1/2 cup	chopped spinach leaves	125 mL
2 tsp	instant minced onion	10 mL
1 Tbsp	butter or margarine	15 mL

Mix all ingredients, 1 tsp (5 mL) salt and 1-1/3 cups (325 mL) boiling water in an ungreased 1-qt (1 L) casserole. Cover and bake in preheated 350°F (180°C) oven until liquid is absorbed and rice is tender, about 30 minutes.
Serves 2

RICE ARMENIAN

Good with shish-kabobs.

1 cup	regular rice	250 mL
1/4 cup	vegetable shortening	50 mL
Dash	Tabasco sauce	Dash
1-qt	milk or beef broth	1 L

Put rice in sieve; set in bowl of water. Rub rice between hands, lifting sieve from bowl and changing water until rice is clear. Drain. In heavy frying pan, melt shortening. Add rice and sauté until golden brown, stirring constantly. Turn into greased 1-1/2-qt (1.5 L) baking dish. Add Tabasco sauce and milk or beef broth. Cover and bake in preheated 350°F (180°C) oven for 30 minutes.
Serves 6

SPINACH SPECIAL

You may even get the kids to try this.

1	package (10 oz/284 g) frozen chopped spinach	1
1 cup	small curd, cream-style cottage cheese	250 mL
1 Tbsp	dry onion soup mix	15 mL

In saucepan, cook spinach in 1/4 cup (50 mL) boiling water (do not add salt) just until tender. Drain thoroughly, pressing out liquid. Stir in cottage cheese and onion soup mix. Heat over low heat, stirring occasionally, until mixture is hot.
Serves 3 or 4

SPINACH ATLANTA

A specialty down in Georgia.

4 lbs	fresh spinach	2 kg
1/3 lb	butter, melted	330 g
1 cup	heavy cream	250 mL

Remove imperfect leaves and root ends of spinach. Wash spinach and drain in colander. In heavy saucepan, boil spinach in water to cover just until tender. Drain thoroughly and chop well. Turn spinach into a 1-qt (1 L) baking dish and pour the melted butter over it. Bake in preheated 400°F (200°C) oven for 20 minutes, or until quite dry. Stir in the cream, and salt and pepper to taste. Replace in oven just until cream is hot.
Serves 6 to 8

SUMMER SQUASH SUPREME

A meld of flavors.

1 lb	summer squash	500 g
	cut in 1/2-inch (1 cm) slices	
3 Tbsp	butter	45 mL
1/2 cup	dairy sour cream	125 mL
1 Tbsp	prepared horseradish	15 mL

In saucepan, bring 1-1/2 cups (375 mL) water to a boil. Add squash and simmer over medium heat, covered, for 3 to 5 minutes, or just until tender; drain. Add the butter, and salt and pepper to taste. Mix sour cream and horseradish and stir into squash.
Serves 4

OVEN-BAKED SQUASH

Easy as falling off a log.

1	package (10 oz/284 g) frozen	1
	sliced squash	
2 Tbsp	chopped onion	25 mL
2 Tbsp	butter	25 mL
4	bacon slices	4
	cooked and crumbled	

In casserole, combine all ingredients with salt and pepper to taste and 1/4 cup (50 mL) water. Cover and bake in preheated 375°F (190°C) oven for 50 minutes.
Serves 3 or 4

ZUCCHINI SESAME

An oriental flair.

1/4 cup	vegetable oil	50 mL
1/4 tsp	sesame oil	1 mL
2	medium zucchini	2
	cut into 1/4-inch (0.5 cm) slices	
2 tsp	sesame seed	10 mL

In large frying pan, heat oils. Add zucchini, sesame seed and
1/4 tsp (1 mL) salt. Cook, stirring frequently, until zucchini is
tender and lightly browned, about 8 minutes.
Serves 4

SAUTÉED ZUCCHINI WITH GARLIC

Don't forget the garlic lovers!

6	small zucchini	6
1/3 cup	olive oil	75 mL
2	cloves garlic, finely chopped	2
Dash	lemon juice	Dash

Cut zucchini lengthwise into three strips each. In frying pan,
heat olive oil. Add zucchini and garlic; sauté quickly until
zucchini is tender but still somewhat crisp, about 5 minutes.
Add salt and pepper to taste and sprinkle with lemon juice.
Serves 6

SIMPLE SCALLOPED TOMATOES

Ready in a flash.

1	can (16 oz/454 g) tomatoes, cut up	1
3 Tbsp	butter or margarine	45 mL
1 cup	bread stuffing mix, cubed	250 mL

In large heavy frying pan, cook tomatoes in butter until hot. Add stuffing mix. Stir 5 minutes, or until heated through and most of the liquid is absorbed.
Serves 4

BAKED SCALLOPED TOMATOES

This recipe comes from Lynn Hoy of St. Thomas, Ontario.

2 cups	canned tomatoes	500 mL
4	toast slices, cubed	4
1 Tbsp	grated onion	15 mL
1/4 cup	melted butter	50 mL

Alternate tomatoes and toast cubes in greased 1-qt (1 L) casserole, ending with toast cubes. Sprinkle with grated onion, and salt and pepper to taste. Pour butter over all. Bake in preheated 375°F (190°C) oven for 20 to 25 minutes.
Serves 4 to 6

TURNIPS WITH CARROTS

Once, long ago, I knew a child who tasted this — and liked it!

1 lb	small white turnips, peeled and quartered	500 g
24	baby carrots (about 3/4 lb/375 g)	24
2 Tbsp	butter or margarine	25 mL
1 Tbsp	shallots or green onions finely chopped	15 mL

Peel turnips and cut into quarters. Trim off stem end of
carrots; peel; place in saucepan. Add water to cover and salt to
taste. Bring to a boil and cook about 7 minutes. Add turnip
quarters and continue cooking until both vegetables are
tender, about 3 to 5 minutes. Drain well. Return vegetables
to saucepan; add butter and shallots and toss.
Serves 4

TURNIP-POTATO PUFF

Can be made fresh or from leftovers.

1-1/2 cups	hot mashed potatoes	375 mL
1-1/2 cups	hot mashed turnips	375 mL
2 Tbsp	butter or margarine	25 mL
1	egg, well beaten	1

Combine all ingredients and salt and pepper to taste in
greased 1-qt (1 L) casserole. Bake in preheated 400°F (200°C)
oven for 30 minutes.
Serves 6

Meats

After his wife had slaved for weeks to prepare a buffet for 50 guests, James called in the guests to show off his wife's work. To allow the cameras to fully capture the beauty of the moment, he took off all the lids, and proceeded to thank his wife by producing a magnum of champagne. He popped the cork. The cork hit the new gift chandelier, breaking it into a thousand tiny glass pieces which drifted uncaringly and haphazardly into the glorious spread below . . .

VEAL VERY VERY

Everyone says this is "very, very good."

3 Tbsp	butter	45 mL
1-1/2 lbs	veal steak	750 g
1	can (10 oz/284 g) tomato soup	1
1 cup	grated cheddar cheese	250 mL

In large frying pan, melt butter. Brown steak on both sides in butter. Transfer to baking dish with the drippings. In saucepan, heat together the soup, cheese and salt and pepper to taste. Pour over the veal and bake in preheated 350°F (180°C) oven for 30 to 35 minutes, or until veal is tender.
Serves 6

VEAL IN SOUR CREAM

This melts in your mouth.

2 lb	veal steak, 3/4 inch (2 cm) thick	1 kg
3 Tbsp	vegetable oil	45 mL
1	onion, thinly sliced	1
1/4 cup	flour	50 mL
2 cups	dairy sour cream	500 mL

Cut veal into 6 to 8 serving pieces. Rub with salt and pepper and roll in flour. In large frying pan, heat vegetable oil. Brown veal pieces on both sides. Place in a roasting pan or casserole and cover with sour cream. Lay onion slices on top. Cover and bake in preheated 350°F (180°C) oven for about 2 hours, or until veal is tender.
Serves 6 to 8

BRAISED VEAL CHOPS

Serve with stuffed artichokes and an orange-and-onion salad.

2 Tbsp	butter	25 mL
2 Tbsp	vegetable oil	25 mL
6	veal chops, 3/4 inch (2 cm) thick	6
3/4 cup	table cream	150 mL

In a large frying pan, heat the butter and oil. Add chops and brown 2 to 3 minutes on each side. Do not crowd pan; it is better to do them 3 at a time. With all the chops back in the pan, salt and pepper them to taste and pour over the cream. Cover and cook over low heat, anywhere from 20 minutes for tender young chops to 40 minutes for older, tough ones.
Serves 6

ANNA'S VEAL CHOPS

A fresh, delicate taste.

4	veal chops (about 8 oz/227 g each)	4
4 Tbsp	butter	60 mL
3 Tbsp	vinegar	45 mL
1/2 cup	chicken broth	125 mL

Sprinkle chops on both sides with salt and pepper to taste. In heavy frying pan, melt 3 Tbsp (45 mL) of the butter and brown the chops on one side for about 10 minutes, or until golden brown. Turn; cook until golden brown on other side. Remove to warm dish. Add vinegar to pan; stir with wooden spoon or rubber spatula to dissolve brown bits. Cook until vinegar has almost evaporated. Add broth and cook briefly until sauce is slightly syrupy. Swirl in remaining butter. Pour sauce over chops and serve.
Serves 4

ROAST SHOULDER OF LAMB

Go-alongs: top-of-the-stove stuffing and sautéed eggplant.

5 lb	shoulder of lamb	2.5 kg
2	cloves garlic, minced	2
1/2 cup	beef broth	125 mL
1/2 cup	dry red wine	125 mL

Rub lamb with a mixture of the garlic, 2 tsp (10 mL) salt and
3/4 tsp (4 mL) pepper. Place on rack in roasting pan and roast
in preheated 400°F (200°C) oven for 20 minutes; pour off fat.
Add broth and wine to pan, reduce heat to 350°F (180°C) and
continue roasting for about 2 hours, basting frequently.
Serves 6

BARBECUED BREAST OF LAMB

May also be fixed on an outdoor grill.

2 lb	breast of lamb cut into 4 pieces	1 kg
1	medium onion, sliced	1
1/2 cup	chili sauce	125 mL
1/4 tsp	red pepper flakes	1 mL

Rub lamb with 2 tsp (10 mL) salt. In heavy frying pan, place
lamb and brown in its own fat. Place lamb into baking pan.
Pour off drippings from frying pan. Add remaining ingredients
and heat 3 minutes. Pour over lamb. Bake in preheated 350°F
(180°C) oven for 1-1/2 hours, or until sauce is almost absorbed.
Serves 4

BARBECUED LAMB RIBLETS

Choose a nice meaty breast of lamb for this recipe.

5 lb	breast of lamb	2.5 kg
1/3 cup	tomato sauce	75 mL
1/3 cup	molasses	75 mL
1/3 cup	prepared mustard	75 mL

Trim excess fat from lamb and cut into finger-size pieces of 1 or 2 ribs each. Place in a single layer on a jelly-roll pan. Bake in preheated 350°F (180°C) oven for 45 minutes; pour off all fat from pan. In small bowl, mix tomato sauce, molasses and mustard; brush part of it over the ribs to coat well. Continue baking, turning once or twice and basting every 15 minutes with the sauce for 1 hour, or until meat is tender and brown.
Serves 4

DEVILED LAMB RIBLETS

The mustard gives this a zesty flavor.

5 lb	breast of lamb	2.5 kg
1/2 cup	prepared mustard	125 mL
4	cloves garlic, minced	4
1 Tbsp	chopped parsley	15 mL

Trim excess fat from lamb and cut into finger-size pieces of 1 or 2 ribs each. In small saucepan, mix mustard, garlic and 2 tsp (10 mL) salt. Place ribs on grill about 10 inches (25 cm) from hot coals; brush with part of the mustard mixture. Grill, turning and brushing several times with remaining mustard mixture, 1-1/2 hours, or until meat is tender and brown. Sprinkle with chopped parsley.
Serves 4

LAMB KABOBS

Rice cooked in clam juice goes well with this dish.

2 lbs	boneless lamb	1 kg
	cut in 2-inch (5 cm) cubes	
1 lb	eggplant, peeled	500 g
	and cut in 2-inch (5 cm) chunks	
3 Tbsp	butter	45 mL
2	large tomatoes, sliced	2

Thread lamb and eggplant alternately onto 6-inch (15 cm) metal skewers. In frying pan, melt butter and sauté lamb and eggplant until golden brown. Place skewers in single layer in shallow baking dish; cover with overlapping tomato slices. Sprinkle with salt and pepper. Bake in preheated 350°F (180°C) oven until tender, about 30 minutes.
Serves 4

LAMB PATTIES

Pass slices of lemon to squeeze over patties, if desired.

1-1/2 lbs	ground lean lamb	750 g
1 tsp	rosemary, crushed	5 mL
6	slices bacon	6
2 Tbsp	shortening or vegetable oil	25 mL

In bowl, combine ground lamb, rosemary, 1 tsp (5 mL) salt and 1/4 tsp (1 mL) pepper. Shape into 6 patties. Wrap a slice of bacon around each patty and secure with wooden toothpicks. Heat shortening or oil in heavy skillet and sauté patties over medium heat until nicely browned on both sides.
Serves 6

ROAST LEG OF LAMB

With mint jelly, of course. . . .

6 lb	leg of lamb	2.5 kg
1 Tbsp	garlic powder	15 mL
1	large onion, sliced	1

Pierce lamb in about 6 or 8 places with skewer; fill holes with garlic powder. Rub lamb with salt; place in roasting pan. Put onion and 1 cup (250 mL) water around lamb. Cover and roast in preheated 350°F (180°C) oven for about 2-3/4 hours for well done, or less, according to taste. Remove cover and roast 15 minutes longer to brown.
Serves 10

BUTTERFLIED LAMB

Start to marinate in the afternoon for the evening's meal.

4 Tbsp	olive oil	60 mL
3	cloves garlic, minced	3
1 tsp	rosemary, crumbled	5 mL
6 lb	leg of lamb,	3 kg
	split open and bone removed	

In small bowl, combine olive oil, garlic, rosemary, 1 tsp (5 mL) salt and 1 tsp (5 mL) freshly ground black pepper. Mix well and rub mixture all over lamb. Put the meat on a broiler rack and cover lightly with waxed paper. Let stand for 2 to 3 hours. Preheat broiler. Remove waxed paper and place lamb on rack 4 inches (10 cm) from source of heat. Broil 15 minutes on each side. Test by cutting a small slit in thickest part. It should be slightly pink inside and nicely browned on top. Slice across the grain on the diagonal and serve with natural juices.
Serves 10

LAMB CHOPS ATHENS

Lemon and lamb are a very compatible pair.

6	lamb chops	6
	about 1-1/2 inches (3.5 cm) thick	
1	juice of 1 lemon	1
1	grated peel of 1 lemon	1

Make incisions in the lean part of each chop and stuff with lemon peel. Sprinkle with lemon juice. Season to taste with salt and pepper and let stand at room temperature for 3 to 4 hours. Broil about 4 inches (10 cm) from source of heat for 10 minutes, turn and broil other side about 6 minutes. Best served immediately.
Serves 6

DILLED LAMB CHOPS

This is best made with fresh dill, but dried will do.

2 Tbsp	vegetable oil	25 mL
4	lamb chops,	4
	about 1-1/2 inches (3.5 cm) thick	
1	can (10 oz/284 g) cream of celery soup	1
1 tsp	dried (or 2 tsp/25 mL fresh) dillweed	5 mL

In heavy frying pan, heat oil. Add chops and brown well on both sides. Lift out of pan and put in a baking dish just large enough to hold the chops in a single layer. Sprinkle with salt and pepper. In bowl, combine soup, 1/2 cup (125 mL) water, and dillweed. Pour over chops. Cover baking dish (use foil if you have to) and bake in preheated 350°F (180°C) oven 35 to 40 minutes, or until chops are very tender. Turn chops occasionally during baking.
Serves 4

EASY SAUERBRATEN

Not nearly as complicated as the old German way.

4 lb	beef pot roast	2 kg
1 cup	Italian dressing	250 mL
1/4 cup	flour	50 mL
1/4 cup	vegetable oil	50 mL
1	large onion, sliced	1

Salt and pepper meat lightly and place it in a kettle. Pour the salad dressing over it. Cover and refrigerate overnight. Drain meat (reserve marinade) and pat dry. Dredge meat in flour and, in a large frying pan with a lid, or a Dutch oven, brown it in oil. Add onion and reserved marinade. Cover and simmer very gently 3 to 4 hours, or until meat is very tender. Thicken liquid for gravy.
Serves 6 to 8

BEEF IN WINE SAUCE

A bachelor's creation, naturally.

2 lbs	stew beef, cut into 1-inch (2.5 cm) cubes	1 kg
1	can (8 oz/227 g) tomato sauce	1
1/2 cup	sherry	125 mL
1	envelope (3 Tbsp/45 mL) dry onion soup mix	1

Combine all ingredients in a 2-qt (2 L) covered casserole. Bake in preheated 325°F (160°C) oven for 2 hours, covered.
Serves 4 to 6

HORSERADISH BEEF BRISKET

I'm a sucker for horseradish.

6–7 lb	fresh beef brisket	3–3.5 kg
4–5 Tbsp	flour	60–75 mL
1/2 cup	chili sauce	125 mL
1/2 cup	catsup	125 mL
1	jar (5 oz/142 g) prepared horseradish	1

Sprinkle the beef with salt (seasoned salt is best) and coat evenly with about 4 to 5 Tbsp (60 to 75 mL) flour. Set on a rack in roasting pan. Roast in preheated 450° (240°C) oven for 30 minutes. In bowl, combine chili sauce, catsup and horseradish; mix well and spoon over meat. Pour 1 cup (250 mL) boiling water into bottom of pan; cover. Reduce oven heat to 350° (180°C) and return meat to oven. Continue roasting about 3 hours, or until meat is tender. If desired, thicken cooking liquid for gravy.
Serves 10 to 12

Ellen T. writes about her niece, who will remain nameless. "As a newlywed," she writes, "she wanted to please her new husband. She knew he liked a cold beer with dinner, so she got one at the store and put it in the freezer to cool quickly. The problem was that it froze, so she put it in the oven along with the roast to bring it back to the right temperature. When she went to take it out of the oven, the explosion singed her eyebrows and the door practically fell off. . . ."

MUSHROOM BEEF BRISKET

You'll want plenty of mashed potatoes to sop up all the good gravy.

4 lb	boneless beef brisket	2 kg
1	large onion, sliced	1
2 Tbsp	flour	25 mL
1/4 lb	mushrooms, sliced	125 g
2 Tbsp	butter or beef fat	25 mL

In large frying pan, brown beef in its own fat. Pour off fat and reserve 2 Tbsp (25 mL) if you're using that instead of butter. To pan, add onion, 1 tsp (5 mL) salt and 1/8 tsp (0.5 mL) pepper. Cover tightly and cook over low heat for 1 hour. Skim fat from pan liquid. Slice meat and return meat and any liquid (from slicing) to pan. Cover and simmer 2 hours. Remove meat to serving platter and keep warm. In cup, blend 2 Tbsp (25 mL) flour with 1/4 cup (50 mL) cold water. Blend this mixture into pan liquid; cook and stir until thickened. Sauté mushrooms in butter or reserved fat; stir in gravy. Pour some gravy over meat; serve remainder in gravy boat.
Serves 6

BEEF STROGANOFF

Serve with buttered noodles and green peas.

1-1/2 lbs	boneless round steak, cubed	750 g
1/2	envelope (2 Tbsp/25 mL) dry onion soup mix	1
1	can (6 oz/170 g) sliced mushrooms	1
1 cup	dairy sour cream	250 mL

Cut fat from meat into cubes and brown cubes in large frying pan until fat is rendered. Remove fat pieces with slotted spoon; discard. Cut meat into 1/4-inch (0.5 cm) strips, 2 to 3 inches (5 to 7.5 cm) long. Add one quarter of the meat to the frying pan; brown quickly. Remove with slotted spoon to bowl. Repeat until all meat is cooked, then return meat to frying pan. Stir in onion soup mix and mushrooms with liquid; heat until bubbly. Slowly stir in sour cream until well blended. Cook, stirring constantly, until heated through.
Serves 6

CHICKEN-FRIED STEAK

This is the way our cook made it when I was a child. Delicious!

1-1/2 lbs	beef round steak	750 g
	1/2 inch (1 cm) thick	
1	egg, beaten	1
1 cup	finely crushed saltine crackers	250 mL
	(28 crackers)	
1/4 cup	vegetable oil	50 mL

With a mallet pound steak into 1/4-inch (0.5 cm) thickness. Cut into 6 serving pieces. In bowl, blend egg and 1 Tbsp (15 mL) water. Have cracker crumbs in pie plate. Dip steak pieces in egg wash and then in crackers. Heat oil in large frying pan. Slowly brown meat in hot oil, turning once. Cover tightly and cook over low heat until meat is tender, 45 to 60 minutes.
Serves 6

PEPE'S TACO STEAK

I think Pepe puts taco sauce on his morning cereal.

1 Tbsp	vegetable oil	15 mL
4	thinly sliced minute steaks	4
	(about 1/4 lb/125 g each)	
1/4 cup	taco sauce	50 mL
1/4 cup	grated mozzarella cheese	50 mL

In large frying pan over medium heat, heat oil. Cut steaks into serving size portions if they aren't already. Add about half the meat to the pan and cook for about 2 minutes per side. Remove to a plate and repeat with remaining meat. Return all meat to the pan; add taco sauce and 2 Tbsp (25 mL) water. Simmer, covered, for about 2 more minutes, turning meat halfway through cooking. Sprinkle cheese evenly over meat and simmer, covered, just until cheese melts, about 1 minute more. Serve immediately.
Serves 4

ANYAH'S CURRIED STEAK

Anyah occasionally helps in my test kitchen, and came up with this one on her own.

1/2 tsp	curry powder	2 mL
4	minute steaks (about 1/4 lb/125 g each)	4
2 Tbsp	vegetable oil	25 mL

In small bowl, stir together curry powder and 1-1/2 tsp (7 mL) freshly ground black pepper. Sprinkle each side of steaks with curry mixture and press into surface of meat. In large frying pan, heat oil. Arrange steaks in pan and cook for about 2 minutes on each side for medium rare.
Serves 4

STEAK AU POIVRE

I prefer the brandy, but rum is good, too.

3 lb	sirloin steak	1.5 kg
2 Tbsp	olive oil	25 mL
1/4 cup	brandy or rum	50 mL

Slash edges of steak and rub all over with salt and pepper. Use plenty of freshly ground black pepper. In large frying pan, heat oil. Pan fry steak over high heat to desired doneness. Remove steak from pan to heated platter. Add brandy or rum to pan. Mix juices and pour over steak. Serve immediately.
Serves 6 to 8

CRACKED PEPPER CHUCK STEAK FOR THE BARBECUE

This makes chuck steak taste like sirloin. Well, almost. . . .

4 lb	chuck steak,	2 kg
	2-1/2 to 3 inches (5 to 7.5 cm) thick	
2 tsp	instant seasoned meat tenderizer	10 mL
3 Tbsp	black pepper cracked or coarsely ground	45 mL

Slash fat edges of steak. Sprinkle all surfaces of steak with meat tenderizer, using about 1/2 tsp (2 mL) per pound/500 g of meat. Do not use salt. To insure penetration, pierce all sides deeply at 1/2 inch (1 cm) intervals with a long-tined fork, working tenderizer in. Press cracked pepper into both sides of steak. Broil steak on grill about 3 inches (7.5 cm) from coals, 35 to 50 minutes, depending on doneness desired, turning frequently with tongs and a turner. To serve, slice with sharp knife diagonally across the grain of the meat at about a 30 degree angle, keeping slices thin.
Serves 6 to 8

"... And then there's the first meal I cooked after I got married," writes Chris E. "My husband came home with a nice sirloin steak. I'd never cooked steak before, so I cut it into bite-sized pieces and boiled it."

A RARE SECRET. . . .

A famous caterer told me how to cook a standing rib of beef so that it will be rare almost all the way through and will stay that way, even with reheating. He said to preheat the oven to 200°F (100°C) only and put the roast in. Start timing it, and roast it exactly 1 hour per pound/500 g. "Then," he said, "you can reheat it at 200°F (100°C) for 1 hour and it will remain rare."

STANDING RIBS OF BEEF, CHINE REMOVED

A simple, delicious recipe.

Standing roast with chine removed, 2 to 3 rib

Arrange roast, fat side up, on rack in shallow roasting pan. If using meat thermometer, insert in thickest part of roast; make sure bulb is not in fat or resting on bone. Season well with salt and pepper. Roast in preheated 300°F (140°C) oven for 2-1/2 hours, or until done to taste. Allow 18 to 20 minutes per pound/500 g for rare; 22 to 25 minutes per pound/500 g for medium, and 27 to 30 minutes per pound/500 g for well done. **Serves 6**

STANDING RIBS OF BEEF, CHINE IN

Use the meat thermometer method.

> 3 rib beef roast, with ribs left in
> 2 cloves garlic, split lengthwise

Cut gashes in fat part of roast and insert garlic cloves. Season with salt and pepper rubbed into the meat. Sear quickly in hot frying pan on top of stove to seal in juices. Make a small incision through the skin of the meat and insert thermometer so that the bulb reaches the centre of the roast. Put into uncovered roasting pan and roast in preheated 300°F (140°C) oven until thermometer registers 140°F (45°C). Serve at once with pan drippings.

Serves 6

Mrs. T.L.H. grabbed the wrong spice can and liberally doused her roast beef with cinnamon instead of pepper. But guess what? Everyone loved it and now she does it that way all the time.

ELEGANT HAMBURGERS FLAMBÉ

Mercy, Maud! How fancy can you get with hamburgers?

1-1/2 lbs	ground beef	750 g
1/4 tsp	marjoram	1 mL
3 Tbsp	olive oil	45 mL
1/2 cup	brandy, slightly warmed	125 mL

In bowl, mix ground beef, marjoram, 1-1/2 tsp (7 mL) salt and 1/4 tsp (1 mL) pepper. Form into 4 patties. Pan fry in hot olive oil in large frying pan, until well browned on each side. Put "steaks" on hot platter. Pour brandy over top, and ignite. Spoon flaming brandy over meat until flames die down.
Serves 4

HAMBURGER AND SPANISH RICE

Easy to make and very tasty.

1 lb	ground beef	500 g
2	cans (15 oz/426 g each) Spanish rice	2
1/4 tsp	garlic salt	1 mL
Dash	red pepper sauce	Dash

In medium sized frying pan, cook and stir meat until brown, pouring off excess fat. Stir in Spanish rice, garlic salt and red pepper sauce. Cook, stirring occasionally, until hot, about 5 minutes.
Serves 4

CARROT-Y HAMBURGERS

A friend came up with this recipe as a way of getting carrots into her children.

1 lb	ground beef	500 g
1/2 cup	grated carrot	125 mL
2 Tbsp	grated radishes	25 mL
1 tsp	grated onion	5 mL

In bowl, mix all ingredients and form into 4 patties. Broil to desired doneness.
Serves 4

BACONBURGERS

The applesauce keeps the meat moist and flavorful.

1 lb	ground beef	500 g
4	bacon slices, cooked and crumbled	4
1/2 cup	applesauce	125 mL

In bowl, mix all ingredients and form into 4 patties. Broil to desired doneness.
Serves 4

SALISBURY STEAK

Go-alongs: broiled tomatoes and buttered carrots.

1 lb	lean ground beef	500 g
1	can (10 oz/284 g) cream of mushroom soup	1
1 Tbsp	Worcestershire sauce	15 mL
	Watercress	

Divide beef into four portions. Pat each portion into an oval
cake about 1 inch (2.5 cm) thick. Pan fry or broil in oven for
about 5 minutes on each side. Meanwhile, in saucepan, heat
undiluted cream of mushroom soup with Worcestershire sauce.
Serve "steaks" topped with sauce and watercress.
Serves 4

NUTTY HAMBURGERS

Good with sliced tomatoes, lettuce, and french fries.

1 lb	lean ground beef	500 g
1/4 cup	chopped walnuts	50 mL
1/4 cup	melted butter	50 mL

In mixing bowl, combine beef, walnuts, 3/4 tsp (4 mL) salt and
1/4 tsp (1 mL) pepper. Mix well; shape into 4 patties. Place
on broiler pan; broil 4 inches (10 cm) from source of heat for
2 to 3 minutes on each side, or until done according to taste.
Arrange on serving dish, top with melted butter.
Serves 4

HONEY SPARERIBS

You may add 1/2 tsp (2 mL) crumbled dried rosemary to the sauce if you like that flavor.

3 lbs	pork spareribs	1.5 kg
1/4 cup	honey	50 mL
1/4 cup	prepared mustard	50 mL
3 Tbsp	vegetable oil	45 mL

Bring a large pot of water to a boil. Add spareribs and cook, over low heat, covered, about 45 minutes, or until ribs are tender and no longer pink inside. Drain and pat dry. In bowl, combine remaining ingredients. Brush ribs with sauce. Grill over medium hot coals 15 to 20 minutes, basting frequently with sauce.
Serves 4

SKILLET SPARERIBS

Make these in your large electric frying pan.

3 lbs	pork spareribs	1.5 kg
1/2 cup	Worcestershire sauce	125 mL
2 Tbsp	fancy molasses	25 mL
1/2 cup	soy sauce	125 mL

Cut spareribs into pieces of 2 or 3 bones each and sprinkle generously with freshly ground black pepper. Place fat side down in large electric frying pan. Fry slowly on both sides until lightly browned. Drench with Worcestershire sauce to taste and sprinkle with salt (garlic salt is best). Cover and turn heat to low. Braise for 20 minutes. Uncover; drizzle with molasses, and soy sauce to taste. Fry about 10 minutes longer, turning ribs often until outside is crispy. Add 1 Tbsp (15 mL) of water or fruit juice to the pan if necessary to prevent scorching.
Serves 4

CURRIED SAUSAGE

Go-alongs: Hot biscuits, honey and canned peaches.

1-1/2 lbs	link sausage	750 g
2 cups	cooked rice	500 mL
1	can (28 oz/795 g) tomatoes	1
1/2 tsp	curry powder	2 mL

In frying pan, partially cook sausages. Cut into pieces. Combine sausage pieces and remaining ingredients, and salt and pepper to taste in a greased 2-qt (2 L) baking dish. Bake in preheated 325°F (160°C) oven for 1-1/2 hours.
Serves 4 to 6

BANANA BAKED SAUSAGES

I first ate these in Jamaica, for breakfast.

8 bananas, unpeeled
8 or 16 link sausages

Slit each banana lengthwise from tip to tip to form a pocket, being careful not to cut through the skin on the under side. Place 1 or 2 sausages in the opening of each banana. Arrange bananas in baking dish, slit side up, and bake in preheated 375°F (190°C) oven 15 to 20 minutes. To brown sausages, place under a broiler for about 3 minutes after baking, or brown them in a frying pan before putting them into the bananas.
Serves 8

ROAST PORK AND 'TATERS

Serve with green peas and fruit salad.

1/2 tsp	ground sage	2 mL
1/4 tsp	garlic powder	1 mL
2-1/2 lbs	pork loin roast	1.5 kg
4	medium potatoes, cut in wedges	4

In small bowl, mix 1 tsp (5 mL) salt, sage, 1/4 tsp (1 mL) pepper and garlic powder. Rub on roast. Place on rack in shallow roasting pan. Roast in preheated 325°F (160°C) oven 1-1/2 hours. Add potatoes; baste with pan drippings. Roast 1 to 1-1/2 hours longer, basting potatoes occasionally, until potatoes are tender and meat thermometer, inserted in centre of roast, registers 170°F (75°C). Let stand 10 minutes before slicing.
Serves 4, with meat leftovers

CHERRY PORK ROAST

This luscious dish comes from my good friend, Virginia Sue Moore.

5 to 6 lb	boneless pork loin roast (double loin, rolled, tied)	2.5 to 3 kg
1	can (21 oz/596 g) cherry pie filling	1
1/2 cup	golden raisins	125 mL
1/2 tsp	ground cinnamon	2 mL

Place roast on rack in shallow roasting pan. Insert meat thermometer so bulb is in center of thickest part of meat. Roast, uncovered, in preheated 325°F (160°C) oven for 2-1/2 to 3 hours, or until meat thermometer registers 170°F (75°C) (allowing 30 to 35 minutes per pound/500 g). Meanwhile, in bowl, combine cherry pie filling, raisins and cinnamon. Spoon cherry glaze over roast several times during the last 20 minutes of cooking time. Remove meat from oven. Let stand 10 minutes before carving. Heat remaining glaze and serve with roast.
Serves 8 to 10

MARNIE'S PEAMEAL BACON

Marnie served us this with home-fried potatoes, sliced tomatoes, and asparagus.

1 lb	peameal bacon	500 g
1/4 cup	grapefruit juice	50 mL
1/4 cup	maple syrup	50 mL
1/4 tsp	dry mustard	1 mL

Place bacon in a small shallow baking dish. In small bowl,
whisk together grapefruit juice, maple syrup and mustard;
pour over bacon. Bake, uncovered, in preheated 350°F (180°C)
oven for 40 to 50 minutes, basting often with the glaze. Increase oven temperature to 450°F (240°C) and bake about
15 minutes more, basting frequently with the glaze. Slice bacon
and spoon remaining glaze over top.
Serves 4

PERFECT PEAMEAL ROAST

Go-alongs: baked acorn squash, and fried apples and onions.

3-1/2 lbs	peameal bacon	1.75 kg
2	pineapple rings	2
	Whole cloves	
1/4 cup	maple syrup	50 mL

Place bacon, fat side up, on a rack in a shallow roasting pan.
Bake in preheated 325°F (160°C) oven for 2-1/2 hours, or until
a meat thermometer inserted in the center registers 170°F
(75°C). Score meat. Cut pineapple rings into pieces and spear
with cloves to top and sides of meat. (If clove stems are too
short, use wooden toothpicks to hold pineapple to meat.) Pour
maple syrup over meat and bake 10 minutes longer.
Serves 6 to 8

PORK CHOPS ORIENTAL

Serve with – what else? – fluffy rice and a green veggie.

1 cup	soy sauce	250 mL
1/4 cup	dry sherry	50 mL
2	small pieces crystallized ginger	2
8	loin pork chops 1-1/2 inches (3.5 cm) thick	8

In small saucepan, combine soy sauce, sherry and ginger.
Bring to a boil and simmer 5 minutes. Cool. Pour over pork
chops in ovenproof baking dish and marinate in refrigerator for
several hours. Then transfer to preheated 300°F (140°C) oven
and bake chops in the marinade for 1 hour.
Serves 8

BREADED PORK CHOPS

Go-alongs: hot cinnamon apple sauce and home-fried potatoes.

6	loin pork chops 1 inch (2.5 cm) thick	6
3/4 cup	fine bread crumbs	175 mL
1	egg, beaten	1
1/4 cup	milk	50 mL

Slash edges of pork chops to prevent curling. In pie plate,
combine bread crumbs, 1 tsp (5 mL) salt and 1/8 tsp (0.5 mL)
pepper. In shallow bowl, beat egg and add milk. Dip chops in
liquid and then in bread crumbs. In greased frying pan, brown
chops on both sides, then place them in a shallow baking dish
and add 1/4 cup (50 mL) boiling water. Cover and bake in
preheated 400°F (200°C) oven for about 50 minutes, or until
chops are tender.
Serves 6

CRANBERRY-GLAZED HAM

A beautiful centerpiece for a gala Easter dinner.

8 to 10 lb	smoked ham	4 to 5 kg
24	long-stemmed whole cloves	24
1	can (1 lb/500 g) jellied cranberry sauce	1
1/2 cup	brown sugar, firmly packed	125 mL

Bake ham according to processor's directions. About
30 minutes before ham is done, score fat with sharp knife and
stud with cloves. Pour off fat from pan; return ham to pan.
Crush cranberry sauce with fork and mix with brown sugar.
Spread over ham. Bake for 30 minutes longer, basting
occasionally. Spoon sauce from bottom of pan over ham.
Serves 12 to 16

HAM STEAKS WITH CRANBERRIES

Serve with hot potato salad and fresh asparagus.

2 cups	raw cranberries, split	500 mL
1 cup	honey	250 mL
2	ham steaks (1 lb/500 g each)	2
	1 inch (2.5 cm) thick	
6	whole cloves	6

In bowl, mix cranberries and honey. Place one slice of the ham
in a shallow baking pan and spread with half the cranberries.
Insert cloves around the edges of the second slice of ham and
place it on top of the first slice. Spread with the remaining
berries. Cover baking dish and bake in preheated 350°F (180°C)
oven for 1-1/2 hours, basting several times with pan juices.
Serves 6

BROILED HAM STEAK

I remember Mama serving this with hot cornbread, sliced tomatoes and corn on the cob.

2 lb	ham steak, 1 inch (2.5 cm) thick	1 kg
1 tsp	prepared mustard	5 mL
1 Tbsp	lemon juice	15 mL
1/4 cup	grape jelly	50 mL

Slash fat around edges of ham. Place on broiler rack and broil, about 3 inches (7.5 cm) from source of heat, 10 to 12 minutes. Meanwhile, in small bowl, combine mustard, lemon juice and grape jelly. Turn ham, spread with mixture and broil 8 to 10 minutes more, or until richly glazed.
Serves 6

HAM WITH RAISIN SAUCE

Serve with baked potatoes and fresh Brussels sprouts.

2 lb	ham steak, 1 inch (2.5 cm) thick	1 kg
1	envelope (1-1/2 oz/43 g) brown gravy mix	1
1 cup	apple juice	250 mL
3 Tbsp	raisins	45 mL

In saucepan, dissolve brown gravy mix in apple juice. Add raisins and bring to a boil, stirring constantly. Reduce heat and simmer 5 minutes. Meanwhile, slash edges of ham steak. Place it in a large frying pan and sauté in its own fat until heated through. Top with sauce and serve.
Serves 6

FREIDA'S HAM DISH

Freida says this is an old Mennonite recipe.

6	country ham portion-sized slices	6
3	medium onions	3
1/2 cup	sour cream	125 mL
1 lb	broad noodles, cooked and drained	500 g

In large frying pan, fry slices of ham until nicely browned.
Remove ham and keep warm. Slice onions and add to ham drippings. Fry until slightly browned. Add sour cream. Let come to a boil and pour over hot noodles. Serve with ham.
Serves 6

FRIED HAM WITH CREAM SAUCE

Serve with hominy grits and sliced tomatoes.

6	country ham portion-sized slices	6
2 Tbsp	shortening	25 mL
1 cup	rich milk or half and half	250 mL

Roll ham in flour seasoned with pepper; no salt is necessary
since ham is salty. Melt shortening in large frying pan and
brown ham on both sides. Pour milk over ham and cover frying
pan. Simmer 10 minutes.
Serves 6

BROILED LIVER

Make sure the liver is at least 1/2 inch (2.5 cm) thick; otherwise it will be tough.

4 Tbsp	soft butter	60 mL
3/4 tsp	savory or tarragon, crushed	4 mL
1 lb	beef or calf's liver	500 g

In small bowl, combine soft butter and savory or tarragon with 1/2 tsp (2 mL) salt and 1/4 tsp (1 mL) pepper. Preheat broiler. Place liver on rack in broiler pan and broil about 3 inches (7.5 cm) from source of heat for about 2 minutes on each side, depending on thickness of liver. DO NOT OVERCOOK. Top each serving with some of the seasoned butter.
Serves 4

VENETIAN LIVER

Serve with crisp bacon slices and sliced ripe tomatoes.

1 lb	beef or calf's liver	500 g
4 Tbsp	vegetable oil	60 mL
4	medium onions, thinly sliced	4

Cut the liver into matchstick pieces with scissors or sharp knife. Heat the oil in a large frying pan. Add onions and cook, stirring often, over medium heat until soft and lightly browned. Push onions to the side of the pan, turn the heat up, and sauté the liver for about 1 minute, or until it turns from red to brown. Sprinkle with salt and pepper just before serving.
Serves 4

LIVER SUPREME

You won't believe you are eating pork liver!

1 lb	pork liver	500 g
	cut into 1-1/2 inch (3.5 cm) pieces	
1/2 cup	flour	125 mL
2	large onions, thinly sliced	2
1	can (28 oz/795 g) tomatoes	1
1-1/2 tsp	grated nutmeg	7 mL

In a brown paper or plastic bag, place 1/2 cup (125 mL) flour,
1 tsp (5 mL) salt and 1/4 tsp (1 mL) pepper. Add the liver a
little at a time and shake well. In a small roasting pan, put
a layer of liver, a layer of onions and a layer of tomatoes.
BARELY cover with water and sprinkle with nutmeg. Bake in a
preheated 350°F (180°C) oven for about 2 hours, or until a
thick gravy has formed. The nutmeg masks the liver flavor and
the result is delicious.
Serves 4

SAUTÉED CALF'S LIVER

This is good served on hot buttered toast.

1/2 cup	shortening	125 mL
2	large onions, thinly sliced	2
2 lbs	calf's liver	1 kg
	cut into small, thin slices	
1/4 tsp	dried marjoram	1 mL

In large frying pan, heat shortening and sauté onions until
they are light brown. Increase heat and add liver, marjoram
and 1/2 tsp (2 mL) pepper. Sauté the liver for 3 to 4 minutes,
stirring constantly. The liver is done when the red juices have
evaporated. Season with salt JUST BEFORE SERVING.
Serves 6

LIVER FROM THE GRILL

When even your grill is tired of hamburgers. . . .

1/4 cup	red wine vinegar	50 mL
1/4 cup	vegetable oil	50 mL
4	small garlic cloves, crushed	4
1 lb	calf's liver, cut into 4 pieces	500 g

In small bowl, mix vinegar with oil and garlic; set aside.
Preheat barbecue and grease grill. Place liver on grill about
4 inches (10 cm) from hot coals. Brush with vinegar mixture.
Barbecue for 5 minutes, brushing with vinegar mixture and
turning once or twice during cooking.
Serves 4

BACHELOR BILL'S LIVER AND ONIONS

"The easier the better," says Bill.

1-1/2 lbs	calf's liver, cut into thin slices	750 g
3 Tbsp	butter	45 mL
1	can (10-1/2 oz/298 g) onion gravy	1
2 Tbsp	chili sauce	25 mL

Brown liver in butter in large frying pan over high heat. Add
gravy and chili sauce. Cover and simmer about 10 minutes, or
just until liver is tender.
Serves 4

Poultry

Two Christmases ago Sharon C. decided to clean the oven so her husband, who usually does the cooking, could roast the Christmas turkey. Sharon didn't bother to remove a pan of bacon grease in the oven; she just turned it to self-clean. Sharon and her husband had unexpected company for Christmas. The local fire department. Unfortunately, the oven door blew off. Fortunately no one was hurt. Fortunately Sharon is not allowed in the kitchen except under strict supervision. Fortunately.

BASIC BROILED CHICKEN

Be sure the chicken is about 6 inches (15 cm) from the source of heat.

2	frying chickens (about 2 lbs/1 kg each), halved and quartered	2
1/4 cup	melted butter, or vegetable oil	50 mL

Wash chickens and pat dry. Sprinkle with salt and pepper and brush with melted butter or oil. Place chickens, skin side down, on rack in broiler pan and broil 6 inches (15 cm) from source of heat for 20 to 25 minutes, brushing occasionally with the butter or oil. Turn chicken, brush with butter or oil, and broil 15 to 20 minutes longer, or until nicely browned. If chickens brown too quickly, reduce heat or move them farther away from the broiler unit.
Serves 4

BASIC FRIED CHICKEN

There are as many recipes for fried chicken as there are cook books, it seems to me. But this is my favorite; it's crispy-crunchy.

1 cup	vegetable oil	250 mL
1/4 cup	milk	50 mL
3 lbs	frying chicken, cut up	1.5 kg
1 cup	all-purpose flour	250 mL

In large frying pan over medium high heat, heat 1/4 inch (0.5 cm) vegetable oil until hot. Meanwhile, pour milk into a deep plate. On a sheet of waxed paper, combine flour, 1 tsp (5 mL) salt and 1/4 tsp (1 mL) pepper. Dip chicken pieces in milk, then in flour mixture. Place chicken pieces, skin side up, in hot oil; cook about 5 minutes or until underside is golden. Reduce heat to low; cook 5 minutes longer. With spatula,

loosen chicken from pan bottom. Turn chicken, skin side down. Cook over medium high heat about 5 minutes, or until skin side is golden brown; reduce heat and cook 5 minutes longer, or until chicken is brown and crispy.
Serves 4

SOUTHERN BUTTERMILK BAKED CHICKEN

That's what I love about the south. . . .

3 lbs	frying chicken, cut up	1.5 kg
1 cup	buttermilk	250 mL
3/4 cup	cornflake crumbs	175 mL
1/4 cup	chopped parsley	50 mL

In a pie plate in which you have poured the buttermilk, dip chicken pieces to coat evenly. In another pie plate, put the cornflake crumbs, 1 tsp (5 mL) salt and 1/4 tsp (1 mL) pepper (seasoned salt and seasoned pepper are best), and the parsley; mix well. Dip chicken pieces in this mixture to coat evenly. Arrange chicken pieces, skin side up, in 13 × 9 × 2-inch (3 L) baking pan. Bake in preheated 375°F (190°C) oven for 45 minutes, or until chicken is golden and crust is crisp.
Serves 4

Lorraine H.'s husband, Dick, bought two turkeys on sale and managed to burn both of them weeks apart — one in the conventional oven and one in the microwave oven. Lorraine says she is known as "the lady with the burned turkeys" and her husband is known simply as "turkey".

CORNMEAL FRIED CHICKEN

This makes the coating extra special.

3 lbs	frying chicken, cut up	1.5 kg
1 cup	cornmeal	250 mL
3 Tbsp	butter	45 mL
3 Tbsp	vegetable oil	45 mL

Wash chicken but do not dry; set aside. In pie plate, mix cornmeal, 1 tsp (5 mL) salt and 1/2 tsp (2 mL) pepper. Roll wet chicken in cornmeal mixture, making sure to coat evenly on all sides. In large frying pan, heat butter and oil over high heat. Add chicken and brown on all sides, about 10 minutes on each side. Reduce heat to low and cook 25 to 40 minutes, turning as necessary to cook on all sides.
Serves 4

QUICK CHICKEN CACCIATORE

Serve with spaghetti. Don't forget the garlic bread.

3 lbs	frying chicken, cut up	1.5 kg
1	medium onion, chopped	1
1	jar (14 oz/398 g) spaghetti sauce with mushrooms and green peppers	1
1/2 tsp	dried basil, crumbled	2 mL

Wash chicken and dry well. Place pieces, skin side down, in large frying pan over low heat; do not add fat. Cook chicken slowly in its own fat until skin side is a rich brown, about 10 minutes. Turn; brown other side. Push chicken to one side. Sauté onions in drippings until soft. Stir in spaghetti sauce and basil; cover and simmer 20 minutes. Adjust seasoning by adding salt and pepper if necessary.
Serves 4

AUNT MAUDIE'S CHICKEN

Aunt Maudie was still looking for "Mr. Right" when she went to her just reward at the age of 82.

3 lbs	frying chicken, cut up	1.5 kg
1	can cream of mushroom soup	1
1	large onion, chopped	1
1	can (4 oz/115 g) mushrooms, undrained	1

Arrange chicken in a single layer in a greased shallow baking dish. In bowl, combine mushroom soup, onion, mushrooms and their liquid, and 1/4 cup (50 mL) water. Spoon over chicken pieces. Bake in preheated 375°F (190°C) oven for 1 hour, or until chicken is tender and richly browned.
Serves 4

STUFFED CHICKEN BREASTS

This is nice enough for a very special occasion. My daughter made it for me on Mother's Day.

4	slices boiled ham	4
4	whole breasts of chicken, butterflied	4
4	slices Swiss cheese	4
	Butter	

Place a slice of ham and a slice of cheese on each chicken breast. Roll together and tuck in edges. Place in a shallow buttered baking dish. Dot with additional butter and a pinch of poultry seasoning if you have it. Bake in preheated 350°F (180°C) oven for 1 hour, or until tender.
Serves 4

AUNT DOLLY'S DRUMSTICKS

My aunt Dolly Holland is a terrific cook. Pretty as a picture, too, at a very young 85 years old.

8	chicken drumsticks (about 1-3/4 lbs/1.75 kg)	8
2 Tbsp	orange juice concentrate	25 mL
5 Tbsp	seasoned bread crumbs	75 mL
1/2 tsp	paprika	2 mL

Puncture chicken skin all over with a two-tined fork. Brush chicken with orange juice (use more if you need it). Spray a non-stick jellyroll pan with cooking spray. Combine bread crumbs, salt and pepper to taste, and paprika in a plastic or brown paper bag. Add chicken and shake well to coat lightly. Arrange chicken in single layer in pan. Bake in preheated 450°F (240°C) oven for 30 minutes without turning, or until crisp and golden brown. Blot with paper toweling and serve at once.
Serves 4

GRILLED GINGER CHICKEN

Something different for the barbecue.

4	chicken breasts, halved	4
3 Tbsp	sesame seeds	45 mL
1 tsp	ground ginger	5 mL
1/2 cup	vegetable oil	125 mL

Wash chicken; dry well. Place chicken in a large shallow dish. Crush 1-1/2 Tbsp (20 mL) of the sesame seeds; mix with ginger, 1/4 tsp (1 mL) salt and a dash of pepper, and oil. Pour over chicken; turn chicken over to coat with marinade. Cover, refrigerate at least 1 hour. Remove chicken from marinade. Add remaining sesame seeds to marinade. Grill chicken, skin side up, 6 inches (15 cm) from hot coals for 15 minutes. Turn, brush with marinade and grill 20 minutes longer, brushing with marinade often.
Serves 4

GARLIC-LEMON CHICKEN

For best results, make the sauce a day before using.

1 cup	butter or margarine	250 mL
1 cup	fresh lemon juice	250 mL
2	envelopes (1-1/2 oz/43 g each) garlic salad dressing mix	2
2	frying chickens (about 3-1/2 lbs/1.75 kg each), split	2

In small saucepan, melt butter. Blend in lemon juice and salad dressing mix; cool; cover and refrigerate until using. Brush chicken with sauce on both sides. Place skin side down on broiler pan set 7 to 8 inches (17 to 20 cm) from source of heat. Broil 15 minutes, turn, brush with marinade and broil 15 minutes longer, brushing once more with marinade, until richly browned. Test chicken for doneness by making a slit near the hip joint. If juices run clear, chicken is done. If juices run pink, broil another 3 to 5 minutes, or until juices DO run clear.
Serves 4 generously

"I loaded up all of my chicken, spices, maple syrup, etc., and took them out to the barbecue," writes William B. "I coated the chicken with the syrup and spices, and when everything was going well, I went off to watch a tennis game. When I returned, the syrup I had left in a plastic basin on the top rack of the grill had melted and all that goo had run down on top of the chicken. It was BLACK! The funny thing is, when all the black was scraped off, the chicken was delicious. I guess you could say that was the start of Cajun Chicken."

BEER-BATTER FRIED CHICKEN

Don't take any short cuts; follow recipe exactly.

1-3/4 cups	sifted all-purpose flour	425 mL
1	can (12 oz/340 g) beer	1
2 cups	vegetable oil	500 mL
2	frying chickens (about 3 lbs/1.5 kg each), cut up	2

In medium bowl, combine flour, 1-1/2 tsp (7 mL) salt and
1/2 tsp (2 mL) pepper. Beat in beer with a wire whisk or rotary
beater until smooth. LET STAND 30 MINUTES. In large frying
pan, pour vegetable oil to 1 inch (2.5 cm) depth. Heat to 375°F
(190°C) on a deep fat thermometer, or until a cube of bread
turns golden within about 60 seconds. Dip chicken pieces into
batter a few at a time, allowing excess to drain back into bowl.
Fry chicken pieces, turning once, for 30 minutes, or until
chicken is done. Place on paper toweling to drain. Keep warm
in 250°F (120°C) oven until all the chicken is fried.
Serves 8

CHICKEN HASH SUPREME

Very elegant, for chicken hash!

1	large green pepper, finely diced	1
2	cans (10-1/2 oz/298 g each) cream of chicken soup	2
1/2 pint	table cream	500 mL
3 cups	finely diced cooked chicken	750 mL

In small saucepan, simmer the green pepper in water to cover
for 5 minutes, drain well. In large saucepan, thin the chicken
soup slowly with the cream over low heat. When the sauce is
right, put in the chicken, the peppers, 1 tsp (5 mL) salt and
1/2 tsp (2 mL) freshly ground black pepper. Stir well and continue
to heat until hash is hot. Serve over hot buttered toast if you like.
Serves 4

Marilyn C. says she came home one night to find that her husband, Bill, had already started dinner. In the frying pan was a grayish, pasty-looking piece of dried-up meat which may have started out as a chicken breast. While she contemplated it, Bill asked, "What is that stuff in the plastic bag on the counter — shake and bake?" Unfortunately, no: it was grout leftover from the day before, when she put up tiles in the bathroom. . . .

CHINESE CHICKEN KABOBS

Serve with Chinese pea pods and fluffy rice.

1 lb	boned chicken breasts cut into 1-1/2-inch (3.5 cm) cubes	500 g
1/3 cup	soy sauce	75 mL
1/3 cup	dry sherry	75 mL
2 Tbsp	sugar	25 mL

Thread chicken cubes on skewers; place in shallow pan; set aside. In large bowl, stir together soy sauce, sherry and sugar until sugar dissolves. Set aside half this mixture. Pour remaining marinade over chicken and marinate, turning occasionally, for 1 hour. Broil 6 inches (15 cm) from source of heat, basting occasionally with marinade, 5 minutes. Turn and broil 3 minutes longer, basting a couple of times. Serve at room temperature with remaining marinade as a sauce.
Serves 4

POLLY'S DRUMSTICKS

Polly says her six children love these. She sometimes has to double the recipe.

24	chicken wings	24
1/2 cup	oil	125 mL
1-1/2 cups	fine dry bread crumbs	375 mL
1	package (0.77 oz/22 g) lemon-garlic salad dressing mix	1

Cut tips from wings; freeze for soup later. Separate wings at joint. With knife tip loosen meat from bone at one end of each wing piece; push meat up bone, forming a small drumstick. Brush liberally with oil. In bowl, mix crumbs and salad dressing mix. Coat chicken with dry mixture. Place in a single layer in baking pan. Drizzle with oil just to moisten. Bake in preheated 400°F (200°C) oven for 20 minutes, or until lightly browned. Serve hot or cold.
Serves 6 to 8

TURKEY ENCORE

There's always leftovers. . . .

3 cups	leftover turkey stuffing	750 mL
2 cups	leftover (or canned) turkey gravy	500 mL
2 cups	leftover cubed turkey	500 mL
	Chopped parsley	

Line bottom and sides of greased 9 × 5 × 3-inch (2 L) loaf pan with stuffing 1 inch (2.5 cm) thick, leaving a well in the center for gravy and turkey. Bake in preheated 375°F (190°C) oven about 25 minutes. Heat gravy and turkey and pour into center of stuffing. Sprinkle with parsley and serve from pan.
Serves 4

MORNAY TURKEY

Go-alongs: Fluffy mashed potatoes and baked red apples.

1	package (10 oz/284 g) frozen broccoli	1
8	slices cooked turkey	8
1	package (1-1/4 oz/36 g) cheese sauce mix	1
Dash	paprika	Dash

Cook broccoli according to package directions, drain well and place in greased shallow baking dish. Cover with turkey slices. Prepare sauce according to package directions and pour over top. Bake in preheated 375°F (190°C) oven 10 to 15 minutes, or until hot. Sprinkle with paprika.
Serves 4

TURKEY ROMANOFF

Easy to make; tasty to eat.

1	package (5-1/2 oz/156 g) egg noodles with sour cream and cheese sauce mix	1
3 Tbsp	butter	45 mL
2/3 cup	milk	150 mL
1 cup	cooked turkey, in julienne strips	250 mL

In saucepan, cook noodles according to package directions; drain. Put noodles back in saucepan. Add remaining ingredients, including sauce mix from package and pepper to taste, mix well and heat.
Serves 4

BARBECUED WHOLE TURKEY

This also stays moist and delicious.

9 to 11 lb	self-basting turkey, fresh	4.5 to 5.5 kg
1/2 cup	dry white wine	250 mL
1/2 cup	vegetable oil	250 mL
1 tsp	leaf rosemary, crumbled	5 mL

Truss and balance turkey in center of spit, securing it with prongs at ends. In bowl, combine wine, oil, rosemary, 1 tsp (5 mL) salt and a dash of pepper. Roast turkey over hot coals, basting every 15 minutes or so with the wine mixture, for 4 to 4-1/2 hours, or until juices run clear when the thigh area of turkey is pierced with a fork.
Serves 8 to 10

"I invited some friends to Christmas dinner," writes Ted N., "because I had just bought a cookbook and I was going to be a Chef Supreme. I bought a large duck. I didn't make any stuffing since that would be too complicated. The duck roasted nicely. It turned out beautifully brown and was tender when I poked it here and there with a fork. I proudly took it to the table, and proceeded to carve it. Alas, one small problem: it had not been eviscerated. The guests wound up eating weiners. and I was the joke of the night."

TURKEY BAKED IN FOIL

This guarantees a tender, juicy turkey every time.

10-12 lb	turkey (reserve giblets)	5 to 6 kg
1/3 cup	butter	75 mL
1	stalk celery with leaves, quartered	1
1	large onion, quartered	1

Rub turkey well with butter; sprinkle with 1 Tbsp (25 mL) salt.
Put celery and onion in cavity. Place turkey in center of
2 long strips of heavy duty foil; wrap loosely. Place turkey in
large roasting pan. Roast in preheated 450°F (240°C) oven for
3-1/2 hours. Meanwhile, put neck, gizzard and liver in a saucepan and cover with salted water. Cover, simmer 2 hours.
When turkey is cooked, open one corner of foil; pour liquid over
giblets. Keep turkey in foil until ready to serve. Strain liquid
from giblets; correct seasoning and thicken as desired for gravy.
Serves 12 to 14

BAKED TURKEY CUTLETS

Serve with hot tomato sauce, rice pilaf and hot cornbread.

1	egg	1
2 Tbsp	vegetable oil	25 mL
1 lb	turkey breast steaks	500 g
1/2 cup	packaged seasoned bread crumbs	125 mL

In a shallow dish, whip together the egg and oil. Dip turkey
breast steaks into oil mixture, then into crumbs (on a piece of
waxed paper) to lightly coat both sides. Place crumbed steaks
on non-stick cookie sheet and bake in preheated 425°F (220°C)
oven for about 12 minutes, or until steaks are golden brown
and cooked through.
Serves 4

CORNISH HENS À LA HENRY

Henry is a well known chef-around-town. Invite him over and he'll do the cooking, if you supply the groceries. We are always happy to.

2	frozen Rock Cornish game hens, thawed	2
1/4 cup	butter, melted	50 mL
1/4 cup	vermouth or other dry white wine	50 mL
1 tsp	garlic salt	5 mL

Rub cavities of hens with salt and pepper. Place breast side up on rack in shallow roasting pan. In small bowl, combine butter, vermouth and garlic salt. Brush over hens. Roast, uncovered, in preheated 350°F (180°C) oven for about 1 hour, or until tender, basting with marinade 3 or 4 times.
Serves 2

CORNISH HENS
IN AN ELECTRIC SKILLET

This recipe came with my skillet years ago, and I still use it although I have a different skillet (which I call a frying pan) now.

4	frozen Rock Cornish game hens (1 lb/500 g each), thawed	4
1/4 cup	butter	50 mL

Preheat electric skillet to 350°F (180°C). Melt butter in skillet. Add hens and brown on all sides in hot butter for 15 minutes. Sprinkle hens with salt and pepper to taste. Lower temperature setting to 225°F (110°C). Pour in 1/4 cup (50 mL) boiling water, cover the skillet and continue cooking for 40 minutes longer, or until hens are tender.
Serves 4

LOIS'S TURKEY STUFFING

An inexpensive stuffing which tastes great.

1	loaf day-old bread, cut into cubes	1
3	large potatoes, scrubbed, boiled in their skins, then peeled and sliced	3
4	stalks celery, finely minced	4
1/2 cup	chopped onion	125 mL

Combine all ingredients and pack lightly into turkey. Makes enough to stuff a 14 or 15 lb (7 or 7.5 kg) turkey.

MAME'S MINCEMEAT STUFFING

We're glad to put the blame on Mame for coming up with this one.

1 cup	chopped onion	250 mL
3/4 cup	butter	175 mL
1	jar (28 oz/795 g) mincemeat	1
2	packages (7 oz/199 g each) seasoned croutons	2

In frying pan, sauté onions in butter until golden brown. In large bowl, mix sautéed onions, mincemeat and croutons. Add 3/4 cup (175 mL) water. Toss lightly. Stuff turkey. Place extra stuffing in a greased casserole. Bake in oven during last 30 minutes of turkey's roasting time. Enough for a 10 lb (5 kg) turkey.

Sauces

Harvey F. says: "Not looking too closely to similar containers, I used instant potatoes instead of cornstarch to thicken my gravy. It was a happy mistake — the flavored spuds with my roast were delicious!"

MARINARA SAUCE

2 cups	canned Italian tomatoes	500 mL
1 cup	olive oil	250 mL
2	cloves garlic	2
2 tsp	Italian seasoning	10 mL

Strain the tomatoes through a colander and place them in a saucepan. Add olive oil. Mince the garlic very fine or put it through a garlic press, and place in saucepan. Add Italian seasoning, 1/2 tsp (2 mL) salt and 1/4 tsp (1 mL) pepper. Stir well, cover and simmer for 30 minutes. If it loses too much liquid, add a little water from time to time, but not very much.
Makes 1-1/2 pints (750 mL)

PSEUDO HOLLANDAISE SAUCE

1 cup	dairy sour cream	250 mL
1 cup	real mayonnaise	250 mL
1/4 cup	lemon juice	50 mL

Combine all ingredients in small saucepan and blend and heat over medium heat. Delicious hot over asparagus or broccoli.
Makes 2-1/4 cups (575 mL)

EASY CURRY SAUCE

1 cup	cream of mushroom soup	250 mL
1 tsp	minced onion	5 mL
1 tsp	lemon juice	5 mL
1 tsp	curry powder	5 mL

Combine all ingredients in small saucepan and heat to boiling.
Great over cooked chicken.
Makes 1 cup (250 mL)

LEMON SAUCE

1	package (3 oz/85 g) cream cheese, softened	1
1-1/2 cups	milk	375 mL
1	package (3-1/2 oz/99 g) instant lemon pudding	1

Into blender container, put cream cheese and 1/2 cup (125 mL)
of the milk. Cover and blend until smooth. Add remaining
milk and pudding mix. Blend until combined. Add a little extra
milk if a thinner sauce is desired. Terrific over hot ginger-
bread or spice cake.
Makes 2-1/2 cups (625 mL)

Barbara G. prepared a wonderful Christmas dinner for a pair of elderly ladies and was silently congratulating herself when she picked up a colander and strained gravy all over her feet.

VANILLA SAUCE

1/4 cup	sugar	50 mL
1 Tbsp	cornstarch	15 mL
3 Tbsp	butter	45 mL
2 tsp	vanilla extract	10 mL

In the top of a double boiler over hot water, combine sugar, cornstarch and 1 cup (250 mL) water. Stir until thickened. Remove from heat and add butter, vanilla and a pinch of salt. Try it over toasted poundcake.
Makes 1 cup (250 mL)

NUTMEG SAUCE

1 cup	sugar	250 mL
1 Tbsp	flour	15 mL
1 Tbsp	butter	15 mL
1 tsp	nutmeg	5 mL

In saucepan, mix sugar and flour. Stir in 1 cup (250 mL) boiling water and cook, stirring constantly, until sauce boils gently and thickens. When it has thickened slightly, add butter and simmer for about 5 minutes. Remove from heat and stir in nutmeg. Good over plum pudding or fruit cake.
Makes 1 cup (250 mL)

MAYONNAISE

2	egg yolks	2
1/2 tsp	dry mustard	2 mL
2 cups	olive or other salad oil	500 mL
	Lemon juice	

In bowl, beat egg yolks, salt and mustard with fork, rotary beater, whisk or electric mixer. Very gradually add oil in a thin, steady stream, beating until thickened. Thin to taste with lemon juice.
Makes about 2 cups (500 mL)

QUICK SOUR CREAM SAUCE

3/4 cup	dairy sour cream	375 mL
1 Tbsp	vinegar	15 mL
2	egg yolks, beaten	2

In top of double boiler, mix ingredients well with salt and pepper to taste. Cook over hot, not boiling, water until thick. Serve hot over vegetables.
Makes about 3/4 cup (375 mL)

FIVE-MINUTE CHEESE SAUCE

1/2 lb	process cheddar cheese, sliced	250 g
1/2 cup	milk	125 mL
Dash	garlic salt	Dash
Dash	cayenne pepper	Dash

Heat ingredients in covered top of double boiler over rapidly boiling water for 5 minutes. Remove cover and beat with rotary beater until smooth.

Makes about 1 cup (250 mL)

Lisa M. asks: "Do I qualify as a Kitchen Klutz? In one day I made icing for bar cookies with garlic butter, and managed to drop a quart of hollandaise sauce on my big toe. I feel compelled to write immediately to avoid further embarrassment. I can't wait to flash my membership card!"

Salads And Dressings

"It was my job to make a huge salad for our final dinner at the cottage settlement," writes Margaret P. "And if I say so myself, it was a masterpiece. I reached for the yellow mustard bottle which I thought my daughter had said contained salad dressing, and applied a generous squirt over all the lovely salad makings. To my horror it was dish detergent!"

CHICKEN-GRAPE SALAD

Proof that you don't need 23 ingredients to make a super chicken salad.

3 cups	diced cooked chicken	750 mL
1 cup	seedless grapes, halved	250 mL
1/2 cup	whole salted pecans	125 mL
1/2 cup	mayonnaise	125 mL

Combine chicken, grapes and nuts, and mix with mayonnaise to moisten well. If you have to, serve on greens, but it's sure good on its own.
Serves 4

CRABMEAT SALAD

Another case of simple and delicious.

1 cup	crab meat (or lobster)	250 mL
1 cup	peeled shredded apples	250 mL
1/2 cup	mayonnaise	125 mL

In bowl, combine ingredients and chill well before serving as is or on lettuce leaves.
Serves 4

OLD-FASHIONED COLE SLAW

Like Grandma used to make.

1	can (6 oz/170 g) evaporated milk	1
3 Tbsp	sugar	45 mL
3 Tbsp	white vinegar	45 mL
1	small head cabbage, finely shredded	1

In heavy saucepan, combine milk and sugar with 1/2 tsp (2 mL) salt and 1/4 tsp (1 mL) pepper; stir briskly. Add vinegar slowly. Chill. (Mixture will thicken on standing.) Rinse shredded cabbage in tepid or slightly warm water and drain well. Place cabbage in bowl, cover and chill thoroughly. Toss with dressing.
Serves 4

COLE SLAW FOR THE CROWD

Another favorite potluck dish.

1-1/2	large heads cabbage, shredded	1-1/2
1 Tbsp	celery seed	15 mL
1-1/2 cups	mayonnaise	375 mL
1 cup	dairy sour cream	250 mL

In bowl, combine ingredients with salt and pepper to taste and chill for several hours. Toss well before serving.
Serves 8 to 10

GREEN BEAN AND ONION SALAD

A great dish when carrots and green beans are fresh from your garden.

4	large carrots, peeled and sliced	4
2 lbs	green beans, trimmed	1 kg
2	medium onions, thinly sliced	2
	Italian dressing	

In separate saucepans, cook carrots and green beans in boiling water until tender. In salad bowl, combine carrots, beans and onion rings. Add Italian dressing to taste and toss again. Refrigerate and allow to marinate for several hours, tossing frequently.
Serves 8

SPINACH-RED CABBAGE SALAD

Fix this the next time you're having steaks from the grill.

4 cups	packed fresh spinach	1 L
1-1/2 cups	shredded red cabbage	375 mL
	Blue Cheese dressing	

Wash spinach and discard tough ends. Tear large leaves into 2 or 3 pieces. In large bowl, toss spinach with cabbage and dressing to taste.
Serves 6

TURKISH CUCUMBERS

Try these the next time you're having lamb.

4	small cucumbers, scored	4
1 Tbsp	Dijon mustard	5 mL
1/2 cup	plain yogurt	125 mL

In bowl, mix all ingredients and chill until serving time.
Serves 4

HERRING SALAD

I wonder who came up with this one? Whoever they are, I'm glad they did!

5 cups	lettuce	1.25 L
	torn into bite-size pieces	
2 Tbsp	chopped dill	25 mL
1	jar (7 oz/199 g) herring fillets	1
	in wine sauce or sour cream	

In salad bowl, place lettuce and dill. Strain sauce from herring over greens. Cut herring into bite-size pieces and add to salad; toss.
Serves 6

CARROT-NUT SALAD

Children love this one.

2 cups	grated carrots	500 g
1/2 cup	toasted pecans	125 mL
1	head iceberg lettuce	1
	Cucumber salad dressing	

In salad bowl, mix carrots and pecans. Break lettuce into bite-size pieces and add to salad bowl. Add salt and pepper if desired and drizzle on salad dressing.
Serves 4

WATERCRESS-GRAPE SALAD

Nice for a ladies' luncheon.

3 cups	watercress sprigs and leaves, packed	750 mL
1/2 cup	seedless green grapes, halved	125 mL
3	green onions and some tops, chopped	3
	Creamy garlic dressing	

In salad bowl, place watercress. Add grapes and onions. Toss with salt, pepper and dressing to taste.
Serves 4

RITZY RICE SALAD

Good enough for your best company.

1	jar (6 oz/170 g) marinated artichoke hearts	1
1/4 lb	small fresh mushrooms	125 g
2	medium-size ripe tomatoes	2
	peeled, seeded and diced	
3 cups	cold cooked rice	750 mL

Drain marinade from artichokes into frying pan. Chop artichokes and reserve. Add mushrooms to marinade, cover and cook over low heat for 10 minutes or until mushrooms are tender; remove from heat and cool. In a bowl, mix together artichoke hearts, mushrooms and marinade, tomatoes and rice. Cover and chill for at least 4 hours. Add salt and pepper to taste.
Serves about 6

GRAPEFRUIT-AVOCADO SALAD

Goes well with roast beef.

2	medium grapefruit	2
2	medium avocados	2
1	head Boston lettuce	1
	Italian dressing	

Remove peel and white membrane from grapefruit, lift out sections. Peel, pit and slice avocados. On 6 salad plates, arrange slices of grapefruit and avocado on lettuce leaves. Pass Italian dressing.
Serves 6

AUNT BEULAH'S GINGER PEAR SALAD

This is an original recipe from my late aunt, Mrs. Beulah (E.K.) Kirby of Pulaski, Virginia.

1	package (3 oz/85 g) lemon gelatin	1
6	pear halves, drained	6
12	ginger snaps	12
1	package (3 oz/85 g) cream cheese	1

In bowl, dissolve gelatin in 1 cup (250 mL) boiling water. Add 1 cup (250 mL) cold water and mix. Place pear halves in single layer in 13× 9× 2-inch (3.5 L) glass dish. In small bowl, crush ginger snaps and mix with softened cream cheese. Divide this mixture evenly in the centres of the pear halves. Carefully pour half the gelatin over pear halves and chill until firm. Add the rest of the gelatin and chill until firm. Cut into squares containing one pear half to serve. (If you want to, you can serve the squares on lettuce leaves topped by a dollop of mayonnaise flavored with ginger, but that would be breaking our 4-ingredient rule!)
Serves 6

CANTALOUPE-STRAWBERRY SALAD

Easy and pretty.

12	lettuce leaves	12
1	large cantaloupe, peeled and cut into 6 rings	1
1 pint	fresh strawberries	500 mL
1/2 cup	mayonnaise	125 mL

On 6 salad plates, arrange lettuce leaves. Top with a cantaloupe ring. Fill centers of salad with strawberries, saving 3 or 4. Crush reserved strawberries and mix with mayonnaise. Top each salad with a dollop of strawberry-mayonnaise mixture.
Serves 6

RUSSIAN DRESSING

1 cup	real mayonnaise	250 mL
6 Tbsp	chili sauce	90 mL
2 Tbsp	minced onion	25 mL
1 tsp	prepared horseradish	5 mL

In bowl, mix all ingredients. Refrigerate between uses.
Makes about 1-1/4 cups (300 mL)

THOUSAND ISLAND DRESSING

1 cup	real mayonnaise	250 mL
2 Tbsp	chili sauce	25 mL
1 Tbsp	sweet pickle relish	15 mL
1 Tbsp	finely minced green pepper	15 mL

In bowl, combine all ingredients. Refrigerate between uses.
Makes about 1 cup (250 mL)

ITALIAN DRESSING

1 cup	olive oil	250 mL
1/4 cup	wine vinegar	50 mL
1	clove garlic, minced	1
1 tsp	Italian seasoning	5 mL

In screw-top jar, combine all ingredients and shake well.
Makes 1-1/4 cups (300 mL)

GREEN GODDESS DRESSING

1/4 cup	tarragon wine vinegar	50 mL
3 cups	sour cream	750 mL
1/2 cup	finely minced chives	125 mL
1 drop	green food coloring	1 drop

In large bowl, combine all ingredients. (Optional: Add 1 Tbsp (15 mL) mayonnaise.) Transfer to quart (1 L) jar with screw-top and refrigerate when not in use.
Makes 1 quart (1 L)

VINAIGRETTE DRESSING

6 Tbsp	olive oil	90 mL
2 Tbsp	wine vinegar	25 mL

In bowl, blend ingredients with 3/4 tsp (4 mL) salt and 1/4 tsp (1 mL) freshly ground pepper.
Makes about 1/4 cup (50 mL)

LEMON VINAIGRETTE DRESSING

3 Tbsp	olive oil	45 mL
1 Tbsp	lemon juice	15 mL
1/8 tsp	dry mustard	0.5 mL
1 tsp	finely chopped parsley	5 mL

In bowl, combine all ingredients with 1/4 tsp (1 mL) salt and 1/8 tsp (0.5 mL) freshly ground black pepper.
Makes about 1/4 cup (50 mL)

MUSTARD DRESSING

1 tsp	dry mustard	5 mL
1 Tbsp	red wine vinegar	15 mL
3 Tbsp	olive oil	45 mL

In a bowl, place the mustard. Add vinegar and stir to a smooth paste with a fork. Add oil, 1/4 tsp (1 mL) salt and a pinch of pepper. Put an ice cube in the mixture and stir hard until ingredients are blended. Discard the ice cube and pour dressing over salad immediately. Dressing is best used right away.
Makes about 1/4 cup (50 mL)

CLASSIC MUSTARD DRESSING

1/4 cup	prepared mustard	50 mL
2 Tbsp	sugar	25 mL
2 Tbsp	vinegar	25 mL
2 Tbsp	half and half cream or evaporated milk	25 mL

In bowl, combine ingredients with 1/4 tsp (1 mL) salt, and beat with rotary beater until light and fluffy. Great to use with potato salad, coleslaw or deviled eggs.
Makes 1/2 cup (125 mL)

SUNSHINE DRESSING

1/2 cup	real mayonnaise	125 mL
2 Tbsp	honey	25 mL
1 Tbsp	lemon juice	15 mL
3/4 Tbsp	caraway seeds	11 mL

In bowl, combine mayonnaise with honey and lemon juice. Beat with rotary beater until smooth. Stir in caraway seeds. Great on fruit salad.
Makes 3/4 cup (375 mL)

Fruit

Betty J. explains: "When my husband complained that the jelly on his grape jelly and peanut butter sandwich was rotten, I couldn't understand why — until I checked the jelly jar. It was a jar of purple hair setting gel I had used the night before to roll up my hair."

FRIED APPLE RINGS

Delicious with link sausages for Sunday morning breakfast.

3	large tart cooking apples	3
1/4 cup	butter or sausage fat, or combination	50 mL
1 Tbsp	packed brown sugar	15 mL
1/4 tsp	cinnamon	1 mL

Core apples. Cut ends from apples and slice each apple cross-wise into 4 rings. In large frying pan, melt butter or sausage fat, and stir in sugar and cinnamon. Add a layer of apple slices and cook over medium heat, turning once, until golden and tender but still intact. Stack slices at side of frying pan and cook remaining apples. Serve warm with pan juices.
Serves 4

NELIA'S FRUIT DISH

Serve this with ham steaks and baked potatoes.

1/4 cup	butter or margarine	50 mL
4	medium onions, peeled and quartered	4
2	medium cooking apples, cut in eighths and cored	2
8	pitted prunes, cut up	8

In heavy frying pan, melt butter or margarine. Add onions and sauté, stirring occasionally, about 5 minutes, or until golden. Add apples, prunes and salt and pepper to taste. Cover and simmer about 5 minutes, or until apples and onions are tender.
Serves 4

THREE-FRUIT COMPOTE

I can't tell you how many ounces (grams) in each can because I use whatever is on sale. As long as the ounces are approximately the same, it always turns out marvelously.

1	can Bartlett pears
1	can cling peaches
1	can greengage plums
1	cinnamon stick, broken in pieces

Into a saucepan, drain the juices from the fruits. Add cinnamon stick pieces and boil together to reduce juices and concentrate flavor. Then heat the fruit in the syrup. Serve hot in dessert dishes or chill. Best prepared several days before using.
Serves 6 to 8

CANTALOUPE AND STRAWBERRIES

Serve this at the beginning of the meal, or at the end.

4 cups	strawberries	1 L
3 Tbsp	icing sugar	45 mL
1/4 cup	cream sherry	50 mL
1	large ripe cantaloupe	1

In blender container, whirl enough strawberries to make 1/2 cup (125 mL) purée. Cover and chill remaining berries. Place purée in a bowl and blend in sugar and cream sherry. Halve cantaloupe, scoop out seeds, and remove fruit. Discard shell and cut fruit into bite-size pieces. Mix cantaloupe into purée. To serve, spoon purée into sherbet glasses or bowls. Top with remaining berries.
Serves 6 to 8

BROILED ORANGE SLICES

Another perfect go-along for baked chicken.

6	oranges, cut into 3/4 inch (2 cm) slices	6
5 Tbsp	butter	75 mL
4 Tbsp	brown sugar	60 mL
1 tsp	curry powder	5 mL

Place orange slices on baking sheet. Dot each slice with butter, sprinkle with brown sugar, and dust lightly with curry powder. Broil, about 4 inches (10 cm) from source of heat, until glazed and heated through.
Serves 8 to 10

EASY ORANGE RELISH

A no-cook delicacy.

3	large oranges	3
1 Tbsp	sugar	15 mL
1 Tbsp	wine vinegar	15 mL
2 tsp	instant minced onion	10 mL

Peel oranges and slice crosswise. Place in a bowl. Add mixture of sugar, vinegar and minced onion; toss lightly. Store covered in refrigerator.
Serves 8 as a relish

Mary Ellen M. spent one hot summer afternoon picking strawberries to make a special dessert for her husband. She carefully washed and capped the berries, put the caps and stems into a colander and the berries into a bowl. She then set the colander on top of the counter, and threw the bowl of berries down the garbage disposal. . . .

BRANDIED PINEAPPLE

Invented to top that slice of Easter ham.

2 Tbsp	butter	25 mL
1	can (14 oz/398 g) pineapple chunks, reserve juice	1
2 oz	brandy	57 g
1/2 cup	heavy cream	125 mL

In frying pan, melt butter and lightly brown pineapple chunks. Add 1/4 cup (50 mL) pineapple syrup and brandy. Heat, uncovered, until pineapple is hot. Turn off heat, cool slightly, and add cream. Mix.
Serves 4 or 5

SIMPLE GLAZED PINEAPPLE

A recipe for beginners or any Kitchen Klutz.

8	slices pineapple, drained	8
2 Tbsp	butter	25 mL
3 Tbsp	brown sugar	45 mL

Place pineapple slices in baking pan in one layer. Melt butter in small saucepan and brush pineapple slices with melted butter. Sprinkle each slice with brown sugar. Bake in preheated 350°F (180°C) oven for 45 minutes.
Serves 4

THREE-FRUIT RELISH

This is good with so many things, even fried liver!

2	unpeeled oranges, quartered and seeded	2
2	unpeeled apples, quartered and cored	2
1 lb	cranberries	500 g
2 cups	sugar	500 mL

Force oranges and apples through coarse blade of food chopper, reserving extra juice for another use. Then grind cranberries and add with sugar to other fruits. Mix well and let stand at room temperature several hours to ripen. Store covered in refrigerator.
Makes about 4 cups (1 L)

CRANBERRY-TANGERINE RELISH

This also can be poured into a mold.

2 cups	sugar	500 mL
1 lb	cranberries	500 g
2/3 cup	tangerine, seeded and finely chopped	150 mL

Combine sugar and 1-1/2 cups (375 mL) water in medium saucepan and bring to a boil, stirring constantly. Boil, uncovered, for 5 minutes. Add cranberries and tangerine. Cook 15 minutes, or until berries pop and mixture thickens slightly. Pour into a 4 cup (1 L) bowl and refrigerate overnight.
Makes 4 cups (1 L)

Breads, Cakes And Cookies

"I really am a Kitchen Klutz," writes Dot W. "Mine has been a neverending series of disasters, small and large. One evening while in the middle of a card game one of my guests noticed that my garbage can was overflowing. I was forced to admit that the problem was my rejected bread dough which suddenly, belatedly, decided to rise after all!"

SESAME SEED BISCUITS

This is a specialty of Charleston, South Carolina, where they
called sesame seed "benne" seed.

3/4 cup	sesame seeds	175 mL
2 cups	all-purpose flour	500 mL
Pinch	cayenne pepper	Pinch
3/4 cup	vegetable shortening	175 mL

In a hot dry frying pan, lightly brown the sesame seeds. In a
bowl, sift together the flour, 1/2 tsp (2 mL) salt and cayenne
pepper. Mix in browned sesame seed, then cut in bit by bit the
shortening. Work in about 1/4 cup (50 mL) ice water, or enough
to give it the consistency of pie crust dough. Roll the dough
out to a scant 1/4-inch (0.5 cm) thick on a lightly floured board,
and cut into tiny circles with a cookie cutter or small glass.
Place on cookie sheets and bake in preheated 300°F (140°C)
oven for 15 to 20 minutes. While they are still hot, sprinkle
them with salt. Store in a covered jar and crisp in a slow oven
just before serving.
Makes 4 to 5 dozen

Sharon O. nominated her friend, Carla M. While living
in Cape Breton, Carla made some buns, and substituted
soy flour for the regular flour, thinking anything from a
soy bean would be healthier and not make much difference in the finished product. But what a difference! No
one in the family could bite into the buns. She put them
outside for the crows, but even the crows couldn't get their
beaks into them, and when they got their claws into them
the buns were so heavy the birds couldn't fly. Even a sniff-
ing dog who came along decided he wasn't that hungry. . . .

POPOVERS

Remember to start these in a COLD oven.

4	large eggs, lightly beaten	4
3/4 cup plus 2 Tbsp	milk	200 mL
3/4 cup plus 2 Tbsp	all-purpose flour	200 mL

In a bowl, beat together the eggs and the milk. Stir in the flour and 1/4 tsp (1 mL) salt, and stir batter just until it is combined. Pour the batter into 12 ungreased 1/3-cup (75 mL) muffin tins and set them into a COLD OVEN. Set the oven temperature to 425°F (220°C) and bake popovers for 35 to 45 minutes, or until they are puffed and golden.
Makes 12 popovers

CHEESE BISCUITS

We like these with beef and vegetable soup for supper.

1 cup	grated sharp cheddar cheese	250 mL
1/3 cup	butter	75 mL
1-1/2 cups	all-purpose flour	375 mL
Pinch	paprika	Pinch

In bowl, cream cheese and butter together; sift in the flour and 1 tsp (5 mL) salt. Mix thoroughly, form into a roll about 1-1/2 inches (4 cm) in diameter, wrap in waxed paper and chill for a couple of hours or longer. When ready to bake, slice dough about 1/4 inch (0.5 cm) thick and place on ungreased cookie sheets. Dust with paprika and bake in preheated 400°F (200°C) oven for 6 to 8 minutes.
Makes about 4 dozen

TEA BISCUITS

There are many recipes for tea biscuits — this is my favorite.

2 cups	sifted all-purpose flour	500 mL
4 tsp	baking powder	20 mL
1/2 cup	shortening	125 mL
3/4 cup plus 2 Tbsp	milk	200 mL

Into a bowl, sift flour, baking powder and 3/4 tsp (4 mL) salt. Cut or rub in the shortening until finely distributed. Stir in the milk with a fork. Turn out onto floured board and knead lightly 5 or 6 times. Pat out into a circle, then roll lightly to 1/2 inch (1 cm) thickness. Cut with a floured 2-inch (5 cm) cutter. Place on a greased cookie sheet and bake in preheated 450°F (240°C) oven for 10 to 12 minutes.
Makes 20 biscuits

PEACHY POUND CAKE

Other fruit preserves may be used instead of peach preserves.

1	bakery pound cake	1
1 cup	peach preserves	250 mL
1 pint	vanilla ice cream, softened	500 mL

Cut pound cake lengthwise into three layers. Place bottom layer on a cake plate and spread with preserves. Add second layer and spread with softened ice cream. Add third layer and spread with preserves. Freeze until firm; slice.
Serves 6

WACKY CAKE

Don't double the recipe. If you need to serve more than 6 to 8 persons, make another cake.

1	can (21 oz/596 g) cherry pie filling	1
1	package (1 layer size) white or yellow cake mix	1
1/2 cup	melted butter	125 mL
1 cup	chopped walnuts or pecans	250 mL

In an ungreased 8-inch (2 L) square cake pan, spoon the pie filling, spreading it evenly. Sift the dry cake mix over the cherries in an even layer. Drizzle melted butter over top of cake mix and sprinkle with nuts. Bake in preheated 350°F (180°C) oven for 40 minutes if using a metal pan, if using a glass pan, reduce oven heat to 325°F (160°C).
Serves 6 to 8

CHOCOLATE-ORANGE TORTE

Sumptuous, and so easy to make ahead for company dinner.

1	bakery pound cake	1
2/3 cup	orange marmalade	150 mL
1	can (16 oz/454 g) ready-to-spread chocolate frosting	1

Cut pound cake lengthwise into four thin layers. Place bottom layer on cake plate and spread with a third of the marmalade. Top with second layer and spread with 1/3 cup (75 mL) of the chocolate frosting. Add third layer and spread with the rest of the marmalade. Add fourth layer and frost top and sides of cake with the rest of the chocolate frosting. Chill and slice.
Serve 8

Cheryl B. was a little embarrassed when she went to the doctor for treatment of a burned chest. It seems she inverted the angel food cake out of the pan onto a cake dish. . . .

JEANETTE'S REFRIGERATOR CAKE

This recipe comes from my good friend, Jeanette Cerven.

1 cup	whipping cream	250 mL
1/2 cup	finely chopped chocolate-covered almonds	125 mL
16	double graham crackers	16
8	whole chocolate-covered almonds	8

In bowl, whip 1/2 cup (125 mL) of the whipping cream until stiff. Add chopped almonds. Spread on crackers and stack together to make a loaf. Wrap in waxed paper and chill overnight. Just before serving, whip remaining cream and frost loaf. Garnish with whole almonds.
Serves 4

CHERRY ANGEL CAKE

Perfect for the bridge club ladies – or gentlemen.

1	bakery 8-inch (20 cm) round angel food cake	1
1	can (21 oz/596 g) cherry pie filling	1
1	can creamy cherry frosting mix	1

Trim a 1-inch (2.5 cm) thick slice from top of cake; set aside. Hollow out cake by cutting a deep circle around top about 3/4 inch (2 cm) in from outer edge, then cutting a second circle about 3/4 inch (2 cm) from center hole. Loosen pieces at bottom with a fork and lift out, leaving a shell. Place shell on serving plate. Spoon cherry pie filling into shell; replace top slice. Frost cake with prepared frosting.
Serves 6 to 8

DATE QUICK CAKE

You can sprinkle icing sugar on top of finished cake if you like.

1	package (14 oz/398 g) date bar mix	1
2	eggs	2
1 tsp	baking powder	5 mL
1/2 cup	chopped walnuts	125 mL

Grease an 8-inch (2 L) square baking pan. Mix date filling from date bar mix and 1/2 cup (125 mL) hot water. Stir in crumbly mix, eggs, baking powder and nuts. Spread in pan. Bake in pre-heated 375°F (190°C) oven for about 30 minutes, or until cake springs back when touched lightly on top.
Serves 6

OATMEAL BREAD

A do-it-yourself project for your health.

2 Tbsp	sugar	25 mL
1/2	cake or package yeast	1/2
1-1/2 cups	regular oatmeal	375 mL
1-1/2 cups	sifted all-purpose flour	375 mL

In small bowl, dissolve sugar in 1 cup (250 mL) water. Add the yeast and 2 Tbsp (25 mL) of the oatmeal, stirring until smooth. In another bowl, combine the remaining oatmeal, the flour and 1/8 tsp (0.5 mL) salt. Make a well or depression in the center and pour in the yeast mixture. Cover with a towel and set in a warm place for 20 minutes. Blend the oatmeal mixture into the yeast with your hands until a stiff dough is formed. Add a little more flour if necessary. Cover and allow to rise for one hour. Form the dough into 2 small loaves or one large one and place in a buttered loaf pan. Bake in preheated 375°F (190°C) oven for 20 minutes, or until browned.
Makes 2 small loaves

EASY YEAST ROLLS

A short-cut method that is long on taste.

1	package active dry yeast	1
2-1/2 cups	biscuit mix	675 mL
2 Tbsp	butter, melted	25 mL

Dissolve yeast in 3/4 cup (175 mL) warm, 105 to 115°F (40 to 45°C) water. Add biscuit mix and beat hard. Sprinkle more biscuit mix on pastry cloth or counter and knead dough until it is smooth. Pat out dough and divide into 16 pieces. Shape into rolls and place on buttered cookie sheet. Cover with cloth and let rise in warm place for about an hour. Brush rolls with butter and bake in preheated 400°F (200°C) oven for 10 to 15 minutes.
Makes 16 rolls

IRISH SODA BREAD

A go-along for your corned beef and cabbage on St. Patrick's Day.

1 Tbsp	butter or margarine	15 mL
4 cups	all-purpose flour	1 L
1 tsp	baking soda	5 mL
1 to 1-1/2 cups	buttermilk	250 to 375 mL

In large bowl, cut butter or margarine into flour until it is the consistency of cornmeal. Stir in soda and 1 tsp (5 mL) salt. Beating constantly with large spoon or mixer, add enough buttermilk to form a firm ball. Knead dough in bowl several minutes, then form into a ball. On greased, lightly floured cookie sheet, with floured hands, flatten dough to a circle 1-1/2 inches (4 cm) thick. With floured knife cut cross 1/2 inch (1 cm) deep in center. Bake in preheated 425°F (220°C) oven for 35 to 45 minutes, or until top is golden brown and loaf sounds hollow when lightly tapped. Cool slightly on rack before serving.
Makes 1 loaf

"Before baking an angel food cake," writes Maureen N., "I went to the basement for flour. We keep it there in large tins. To assure my cake's light texture, I sifted the flour three times. Thirty minutes later I went to take the cake out of the oven. I couldn't lift the hot pan, it was so heavy! What had happened? Next to the flour tin in the dark basement there was a tin of Plaster of Paris. I had scooped it up by mistake. . . ."

EASY DUMPLINGS

You make the stew; now, we'll make the dumplings. . . .

1 cup	all-purpose flour	250 mL
1 Tbsp	baking powder	15 mL
1-1/2 Tbsp	vegetable oil	22 mL
2/3 cup	milk	150 mL

In mixing bowl, sift together flour, baking powder and 1/2 tsp (2 mL) salt. In another bowl, combine oil and milk; add to dry ingredients only until blended. Drop by spoonfuls over simmering stew or chicken, cover tightly and simmer 15 minutes. Serve at once.
Makes 6 to 8 dumplings

LACY CORN BREAD

This is my Aunt Dolly Holland's recipe (I promised her I would mention her name).

1 cup	white cornmeal	250 mL
1	small onion, finely chopped	1
	Oil for frying	

In a bowl, put 1-3/4 cups (375 mL) cold water. Gradually stir in cornmeal. Add onion, 2 tsp (10 mL) salt and a dash of pepper. Mix well. In frying pan, heat 1/4 inch (0.5 cm) vegetable oil. Drop the batter by heaping tablespoons into the oil and fry, turning once, until rounds are golden brown. Drain on paper toweling.
Serves 6

DOUBLE CORN MUFFINS

These are great served with chicken noodle soup.

1	large package (14 oz/398 g) corn muffin mix	1
1 cup	cream style corn	250 mL
1	egg, beaten	1
1/2 cup	shredded cheddar cheese	125 mL

In large mixing bowl, combine all ingredients (and you can add a dash of hot pepper sauce if you have it handy). Stir until blended. Fill large greased muffin cups two-thirds full. Bake in preheated 425°F (220°C) oven for 12 to 15 minutes, or until muffins are brown.
Makes 10 to 12 large muffins

ONION QUICK BREAD

This is good when you're having a soup and salad supper.

1	loaf french bread	1
1/2	package (3 Tbsp/45 mL) dry onion soup mix	1/2
1/4 cup	butter, softened	50 mL

Split bread lengthwise. In small bowl, combine onion soup mix and butter. Spread on cut sides of bread and put halves back together. Wrap in aluminum foil, leaving foil open a bit at top to keep bread crisp. Heat in preheated 325°F (160°C) oven for about 20 minutes.
Makes 1 loaf

Carol H. tells about the Great Brownie Bust. "In the process of preparing two boxes of brownies, I added the proper amounts of egg and water but accidentally omitted the second package of mix. I discovered this after I had put the pan in the oven and it had baked for about five minutes. I removed the pan from the oven, dumped the forgotten mix into the pan, and attempted to re-mix the whole shooting match. Alas, it wouldn't mix properly so I added chocolate syrup to make it moister and easier to mix. A can of syrup later, I finally was satisfied and finished baking them. Everyone dug in and complimented me on how good they were, but a few minutes later everyone was running for the bathroom. This kept up all night. I still don't know why, but I haven't made any more brownies."

LEMON PARSLEY LOAVES

Designed for the barbecue.

2	large brown and serve french loaves each about 8 inches (20 cm) long	2
1/4 cup	butter or margarine, softened	50 mL
1/4 cup	chopped parsley	50 mL
2 tsp	lemon juice	10 mL

Slice rolls diagonally in 1 inch (2.5 cm) slices. Combine butter and parsley, then blend in lemon juice. Spread one side of each slice with mixture. Reassemble each roll on a long skewer, inserting skewer through center of slices. Broil 3 to 4 inches (7.5 to 10 cm) from very hot coals, turning to brown evenly.
Serves 4 to 6

PEANUT MUFFINS

The kids will love these.

1	package (8-1/2 oz/240 g) corn muffin mix	1
	Milk, as called for by mix	
1/3 cup	chopped salted peanuts	75 mL

Prepare corn muffin mix as directed, stirring in peanuts. Bake as directed.
Makes 12 small muffins

DILLY QUICK BREAD

Watch carefully while broiling so they don't burn.

4 Tbsp	butter or margarine, softened	60 mL
2 tsp	lemon juice	10 mL
1/2 tsp	dried dillweed	2 mL
6	slices french bread	6

In small mixing bowl, combine butter or margarine, lemon juice and dillweed. Set aside. Place bread slices on broiler rack and broil 3 to 4 inches (7.5 to 10 cm) from source of heat until golden, 1 to 2 minutes. Turn, spread butter mixture on untoasted side and broil 1 to 2 minutes more.
Makes 6 slices

Mildred W. is famous for a cookie she invented called Cementies. They were supposed to be regular oatmeal cookies, but they turned out cement-hard. However, the family likes them because, they say, you can gnaw on a Cementie for hours.

TROPICAL CREAM CAKES

A favorite dessert of a 12-year-old neighbor.

1/2 cup	flaked coconut	125 mL
1 cup	frozen whipped topping	250 mL
4	individual dessert sponge shells	4
1	can (5 oz/142 g) vanilla pudding	1

On a cookie sheet in a preheated 350°F (180°C) oven, toast 3 Tbsp (45 mL) of the coconut for 8 to 10 minutes. Cool. Spread whipped topping around the sides and top edges of dessert shells. Sprinkle with toasted coconut. Stir remaining coconut into pudding. Spoon some pudding into the center of each shell. Garnish with a dollop of whipped topping.
Serves 4

SELMA'S SHORTCAKES

Recipe courtesy of Selma Smith of St. Catharines, Ontario.

1	package (10 oz/284 g) frozen crumb cakes	1
1	package (10 oz/284 g) frozen peaches thawed and drained	1
1 cup	frozen unsweetened blueberries	250 mL
1 cup	heavy cream, whipped	250 mL

Split crumb cakes and place bottoms on serving plates. Top with peaches and blueberries, reserving a few pieces for garnish. Spoon a dollop of cream on each; replace tops. Spoon remaining cream over tops and garnish with reserved fruit.
Serves 4

FROZEN SHERBET CAKE

A special occasion cake.

1	bakery angel food cake, frozen	1
2 pints	lime sherbet, slightly softened	1 L
1	small carton whipped topping	1
	Mint sprigs (optional)	

Insert toothpicks midpoint at several places around outside of cake. Using picks as guides, split cake with serrated knife or long thread. With narrow spatula, quickly spread 1 pint (500 mL) sherbet on bottom layer. Then quickly spread remaining 1 pint (500 mL) sherbet on top layer, swirling attractively. Carefully place on bottom layer. Freeze until surface has hardened. Cover airtight and freeze until firm. Remove from freezer 10 to 15 minutes before serving. Garnish with dollops of whipped topping, and mint sprigs if desired.
Serves 10 to 12

Mary M. tells about the time she made a "soldier" cake for her young son's birthday — so big it had to be assembled on a TV tray. Looking for a safe place to keep it until the party, she thought of the oven, so she slipped it in there. Her son, though, had also requested "pigs in a blanket" for his birthday party, so Mom, not thinking, turned the oven to 375°F to preheat it. . . .

DOUBLE CHOCOLATE CAKE

This meeting of chocoholics will come to order.

1	package (2 layer size) devil's food cake mix	1
1	package (4-1/2 oz/128 g) instant chocolate pudding	1
1/4 cup	vegetable oil	50 mL
2	eggs	2

In ungreased 13× 9× 2 inch (3.5 L) baking pan, mix all ingredients with a fork, scraping corners frequently, until moistened. Stir batter hard with a fork for 1 minute. Scrape down sides with rubber spatula. Spread batter evenly in pan. Bake in preheated 350°F (180°C) oven until top springs back when touched lightly in center, 40 to 45 minutes. Cool. Loosen cake from sides. Cut into squares and serve directly from pan. Store any leftover cake loosely covered in the refrigerator.
Serves 8

DREAM COOKIES

You can put a chocolate glaze on these if you wish.

3/4 cup	unsalted butter	175 mL
3/4 cup	white sugar	175 mL
4	egg yolks, well beaten	4
1 cup	sifted all-purpose flour	250 mL

In bowl, cream butter and sugar until light and fluffy. Add egg yolks in thirds, beating well after each addition. Add flour in two batches, blending well each time. Chill well, about 2 hours. Drop by heaping teaspoonfuls (15 mL) onto ungreased cookie sheets about 2 inches (5 cm) apart. Bake in preheated 350°F (180°C) oven for about 8 minutes.
Makes about 5 dozen

BROWN SUGAR MACAROONS

What to make when you have an egg white left over.

1 cup	light brown sugar	250 mL
1 Tbsp	flour	15 mL
1 cup	chopped walnuts	250 mL
1	egg white, stiffly beaten	1

In bowl, mix together sugar, flour and nuts. Fold in egg white. Drop far apart on greased cookie sheet. Bake in preheated 325°F (160°C) oven for 15 minutes. Remove from cookie sheets when partly cool.
Makes about 18 cookies

PEANUT MACAROONS

Good, and inexpensive to make.

1	egg white	1
1/4 cup	white sugar	50 mL
1/2 cup	chopped peanuts	125 mL
1 tsp	vanilla extract	5 mL

In bowl, beat egg white until stiff. Gradually add sugar, beating constantly. Stir in peanuts and vanilla. Drop by teaspoonfuls (15 mL) about 1-1/2 inches (3 cm) apart, on greased cookie sheets. Bake in preheated 300°F (140°C) oven about 12 to 15 minutes, or until dry.
Makes about 16 cookies

MINCEMEAT GINGER COOKIES

Delightful with a glass of cold milk.

1	package (14-1/2 oz/412 g) gingerbread mix	1
1 cup	prepared mincemeat	250 mL
1/2 cup	chopped walnuts	125 mL

Combine all ingredients with 1/2 cup (125 mL) water and mix well. Drop dough by teaspoonfuls (15 mL) about 2 inches (5 cm) apart onto lightly greased cookie sheet. Bake in preheated 375ÉF (190ÉC) oven 10 to 12 minutes, or until no imprint remains when touched in the center.
Makes about 3 dozen cookies

CHINESE CHEWS

I remember making these on a hot plate when I was in college.

1	package (6 oz/170 g) semi-sweet chocolate pieces	1
1	package (6 oz/170 g) butterscotch pieces	1
1 cup	salted peanuts	250 mL
1	can (3-1/2 oz/99 g) Chinese noodles	1

In top of double boiler, combine chocolate and butterscotch pieces. Heat over hot (not boiling) water until smooth, stirring occasionally. Remove from heat; stir in peanuts and noodles. Drop by teaspoonfuls onto waxed paper and allow to cool.
Makes about 36 pieces

EASY SHORTBREAD

The easiest shortbread recipe I've ever come across.

1/2 lb	butter	250 g
2 cups	sifted all-purpose flour	500 mL
3 heaping Tbsp	icing sugar	45 mL
3 heaping Tbsp	cornstarch	45 mL

In bowl, mix all ingredients well and chill until it can be handled. Form into balls about the size of walnuts, place on ungreased cookie sheet and press with a fork. Bake in preheated 325°F (160°C) oven for 12 minutes. Do not overbake.
Makes 2 to 3 dozen

FLUFFY SHORTBREAD

These can be decorated with candied fruit, "sprinkles," etc.

1 cup	butter, well creamed	250 mL
1/2 cup	icing sugar	125 mL
2 cups	sifted all-purpose flour	500 mL
1/4 tsp	vanilla	1 mL

In bowl, beat together all ingredients plus a pinch of salt until mixture is the consistency of whipped cream. Drop from teaspoon onto ungreased cookie sheet and bake in preheated 350°F (180°C) oven for 10 minutes.
Makes 2 to 3 dozen

NUT COOKIES

Try these with black walnuts if you have them.

2	eggs, separated	2
1 cup	brown sugar	250 mL
1 cup	chopped nuts	250 mL
6 Tbsp	flour	90 mL

In bowl, beat egg yolks until pale and thick. Gradually beat in sugar, then add nuts and a dash of salt. In another bowl, beat egg whites until stiff but not dry. Fold them into the first mixture, then stir in the flour. Drop by teaspoonfuls (15 mL) onto ungreased cookie sheets about 2 inches (5 cm) apart. Flatten with spatula. Bake in preheated 350°F (180°C) oven for 5 to 8 minutes, or until firm. Do not overbake.
Makes about 50 cookies

EASY OATMEAL COOKIES

A breakfast of these for the children is better than no breakfast at all.

1/2 cup	bacon bits	125 mL
1	package (12 or 18 oz/340 or 511 g) oatmeal cookie mix	1
1/2 cup	chopped peanuts	125 mL
1	egg	1

In bowl, combine all ingredients and 2 Tbsp (25 mL) water. Mix well with fork. Drop by rounded teaspoonfuls onto greased cookie sheets. Bake in preheated 375°F (190°C) oven for 13 to 14 minutes. Do not overbake.
Makes 3 to 4 dozen

Marjorie W. tells of a cake she made for her mother's birthday once. "Wanting to try something unusual, I decided on a spice cake with a maple syrup frosting. Well, the icing was like glue and the cake flopped completely. Not wanting to hurt my feelings, my mother said she would break it up into pieces and put it out in the back yard near the birdbath for the birds to eat. Later that evening a neighbor came over and told us she had just come back from the vet's office with her dog. It seems Fritzie got real sick after eating something by our birdbath. . . ."

COCONUT-APRICOT BALLS

These are nice at Christmas, and no baking needed.

1-1/2 cups	ground dried apricots	375 mL
2 cups	shredded coconut	500 mL
2/3 cup	sweetened condensed milk	150 mL
	Icing sugar	

In bowl, combine apricots and coconut. Add sweetened condensed (not evaporated) milk and mix well. Shape into 1-inch (2.5 cm) balls and roll in icing sugar. Place on waxed paper to dry for one hour. Store in airtight container.
Makes about 32

Desserts

Writes Dayle T., "Our 12-year-old, Jody, takes the most teasing about her banana bread. Our oven is a convection-microwave combination, and after checking the loaf for doneness, she decided it needed another 15 minutes. By mistake she hit the microwave touchpads instead of the convection controls, and the result was a loaf like a brick. Her laughing father, with an electric saw, cut it into slices, arranged them on a tray and took them to work for coffee break!"

FROZEN YOGURT PIE

Delicious – cool and creamy.

2	containers (8 oz/227 g each) fruit flavored yogurt	2
1	container (8 oz/227 g) non-dairy whipped topping, thawed	1
1	baked 9-inch (22.5 cm) graham cracker crust	1

In bowl, fold yogurt into whipped topping, blending well. Spoon into crust. Freeze until firm, 4 hours or overnight. Remove from freezer 30 minutes, or longer for softer texture, before cutting; keep chilled in refrigerator. Garnish with additional whipped topping and fruit if desired.
Serves 6

ANGEL ICE CREAM PIE

Make it any time; keep it in the freezer.

1-1/2 pints	strawberry ice cream, softened	750 mL
1-1/2 cups	cubed angel food cake	375 mL
1/2 oz	bitter chocolate, (1/2 square) shaved	14 g

Let ice cream soften slightly. Place half of the angel food cake cubes in the bottom of a 9-inch (22 cm) pie plate. Spoon half the ice cream over them. Add remaining cake cubes and ice cream. Smooth ice cream to edges of pie pan. Sprinkle chocolate on top. Cover with freezer wrapping and freeze until needed.
Serves 6

EASY STRAWBERRY TARTS

Of course, any other fruit or combination may be used.

1	package (4 serving size) instant vanilla pudding	1
8	3-inch (7.5 cm) tart shells, baked	8
2 cups	small whole strawberries	500 mL
1	package (3 oz/185 g) strawberry gelatin	1

Prepare pudding mix according to package directions and forget that the milk called for will make a fifth ingredient! Chill pudding, then divide it evenly among the tart shells. Top each tart with strawberries. Prepare gelatin according to package directions. Chill until thickened but not set. Spoon gelatin over tarts, using just enough to cover fruits with a thin glaze. Chill until ready to serve.
Makes 8 tarts

CANDY CAKE SQUARES

Nothing could be more simple.

1 cup	brown sugar	250 mL
1/2 cup	butter or margarine	125 mL
1 tsp	vanilla extract	5 mL
2 cups	quick-cooking oatmeal	500 mL

In bowl, mix ingredients in order given. Turn into a buttered 8-inch (2 L) square pan and bake in preheated 350°F (180°C) oven for 20 to 25 minutes. Cut while warm.
Makes about 12 squares

RASPBERRY SHORTCAKE

Sugared fresh raspberries, if they are in season, should be used.

2	packages (10 oz/284 g each) frozen raspberries, thawed	2
6	slices pound cake	6
6 Tbsp	butter	90 mL
	Heavy cream or sour cream	

Thaw the raspberries. In large frying pan, toast the pound cake slices in the butter on both sides. Remove cake slices to individual plates, spoon raspberries over, and top with cream.
Serves 6

QUICKIE BROWNIES

Whip these up for the children in a flash.

3	squares (3 oz/85 g) unsweetened chocolate	3
1	can (14 oz/398 g) sweetened condensed milk	1
2 cups	vanilla wafer crumbs	500 mL
1 cup	chopped nuts	250 mL

In the top of a double boiler, melt chocolate with milk until smooth. Remove from heat, add vanilla wafer crumbs and nuts. Turn into a buttered baking pan so that batter will be about 3/4 inch (2 cm) thick, and bake in preheated 300°F (140°C) oven for 30 to 35 minutes. Cut into squares.
Makes about 12

BEST RICE PUDDING

No raisins, but this is the best rice pudding I ever tasted.

4 cups	milk	1 L
2/3 cup	sugar	150 mL
1/2 tsp	nutmeg	2 mL
3 Tbsp	raw rice	45 mL

Mix all ingredients and 1/2 tsp (2 mL) salt in a buttered baking dish. Stir well. Bake in preheated 300°F (140°C) oven for 3-1/2 hours, stirring 3 times the first hour so rice doesn't settle. This has a thick, creamy texture and a lovely flavor.
Serves 6 to 8

BAKED APPLE PUDDING

Best, naturally, with the addition of whipped cream.

4	apples, peeled and sliced	4
1/2 cup	brown sugar	125 mL
1 cup	graham cracker crumbs	250 mL
3 Tbsp	lemon juice	45 mL

In bowl, combine all ingredients and 3/4 cup (175 mL) water and mix well. Turn into a greased baking dish and bake in preheated 375°F (190°C) oven for 30 minutes, or until apples are tender.
Serves 4

Joan D. tells about a dessert, ". . . One of my favorites, squash pie. That it was the first time I'd ever made it didn't faze me. But, it was terrible. It stuck to the roof of our mouths and looked like the grand canyon. Then it was pointed out to me that I had neglected to include a few ingredients — like eggs, milk and sugar. I had just put mashed squash in a pie shell."

CREAM PUDDING

This recipe goes way back.

1 pint	dairy sour cream	500 mL
2 Tbsp	flour	25 mL
3 Tbsp	sugar	45 mL
	Cranberry or other fruit sauce	

In heavy saucepan, combine sour cream and flour and mix until smooth. Bring to boil, stirring. Simmer, stirring occasionally, for 25 minutes. Remove from heat and add sugar and 1/4 tsp (1 mL) salt. Cool, then chill. Serve with fruit sauce.
Serves 3 to 4

TIPSY PUDDING

So does this one!

4	eggs	4
1/2 cup	sugar	125 mL
1 cup	sifted flour	250 mL
3/4 cup	rum	175 mL

In a bowl, beat the eggs. Gradually add the sugar, beating until thick and light. Add the flour, mixing lightly until well blended. Preheat oven to 350°F (180°C). Butter 6 custard cups and dust lightly with sugar. Divide the mixture among the cups. Bake for 20 minutes, or until set and lightly browned. Pour 2 Tbsp (25 mL) rum on each pudding and serve cold.
Serves 6

QUICK LEMON DESSERT

Sassy and satisfying.

16	chocolate-covered graham crackers	16
1	package (3 oz/185 g) lemon chiffon pie filling	1
1 cup	heavy cream, whipped	250 mL

Crush crackers; spread half in a 13 × 9 × 2-inch (3.5 L) baking
dish. Prepare pie filling according to package directions;
pour over crackers; cool. Spread whipped cream over filling.
Sprinkle with remaining crackers. Chill.
Serves 4

TROPICAL PARADISE

Don't you just love the flowery names folks give desserts?

1	can (20 oz/568 g) crushed pineapple in syrup	1
3 Tbsp	crushed peppermint candies	45 mL
1 cup	heavy cream, whipped	250 mL

Freeze unopened can of pineapple for at least 5 hours. Just
before serving, fold peppermint candies into whipped
cream. Open both ends of can of frozen pineapple and push
it out in one piece (if necessary wrap hot towel around it to
ease removal). Slice and serve with topping.
Serves 6

Carroll S. remembers the first cherry pie she ever baked. "I followed the recipe carefully," she writes, "and I put it in a 200°F oven because I thought slow baking would result in a tender crust. About six hours later I had a beautiful, brown pie, pretty as a picture. But . . . you couldn't have cut it with a hacksaw. We did eat the filling, as soon as we chipped away the lattice crust."

PEG'S RASPBERRY DESSERT

Nice when the girls get together . . . or the boys . . . or the girls and boys together.

3 Tbsp	cream or dry sherry	45 mL
1	package (10 oz/284 g) frozen raspberries, thawed	1
4	soft macaroons	4
1 pint	vanilla ice cream	500 mL

In bowl, sprinkle sherry over raspberries. Crumble one macaroon in each of 4 sherbet glasses. Top macaroons with a scoop of ice cream; spoon raspberry mixture over.
Serves 4

VANILLA JUBILEE

A mouth-watering flavor.

1	jar (16 oz/454 g) dark cherry preserves	1
1/4 cup	port wine	50 mL
1/4 tsp	almond extract	1 mL
1 qt	vanilla ice cream	1 L

In small bowl, combine preserves, wine and extract. Serve as a sauce over ice cream.
Serves 4 to 6

BLUEBERRY CRACKLE

A pioneer recipe brought up to date.

1	can (21 oz/596 g) blueberry pie filling	1
1	stick pie crust mix	1
1/2 cup	brown sugar	125 mL
1 tsp	cinnamon	5 mL

In an 8-inch (2 L) square baking pan, pour blueberry pie filling; heat in preheated 350°F (180°C) oven for 10 minutes. In bowl, mix pie crust mix, sugar and cinnamon with a pastry blender. Sprinkle this mixture over blueberries. Turn oven to broil and broil for about 5 minutes, or until golden brown.
Serves 4 to 6

TIA MARIA TORTE

Sit back and enjoy the compliments.

1	bag (1 lb/500 g) chocolate chip cookies	1
1/2 cup	milk	125 mL
1/2 cup	Tia Maria	125 mL
2	large cartons whipped topping	2

Dip each cookie first into milk and then into Tia Maria (briefly so they don't get soggy). Place a layer of the cookies in a 9 × 13 × 2-inch (3.5 L) glass dish. Cover with a 1-inch (2.5 cm) layer of whipped topping. Repeat layers, ending with whipped topping. Refrigerate for several hours. Delicious!
Serves 8 to 10

ZABAGLIONE

A classic . . . the pride of Italy.

6	egg yolks	6
1/2 cup	sugar	125 mL
2/3 cup	marsala wine	150 mL
3	large ripe strawberries (optional)	3

In the top of a double boiler, place the egg yolks. Beat, then gradually add sugar, beating until the mixture becomes pale, yellow and fairly thick. Add a pinch of salt. Pour in the wine slowly, beating constantly. Place the pan over boiling water and continue beating until the mixture thickens again. It is done when it sticks to the beater. Pour into 6 dessert dishes and garnish with half a ripe strawberry, if desired. Serve hot at once, or place in refrigerator to chill. Should be eaten within a few hours.
Serves 6

APRICOTS À LA COGNAC

Adults only, please.

1 lb	dried apricots, cut into pieces	500 g
2/3 cup	sugar	150 mL
1 cup	cognac (brandy) to cover	250 mL

In container with lid, combine ingredients and cover. Let stand at room temperature at least 24 hours; flavor is better if steeped 1 week. Serve chilled.
Serves 6 to 8

STRAWBERRY HEAVEN

Be sure to let it chill properly.

1	package (3 oz/85 g) strawberry gelatin	1
1 pint	strawberry ice cream	500 mL
8 oz	(half a 16 oz/454 g cake) angel food cake	227 g
8	fresh strawberries (optional)	8

In bowl, dissolve gelatin in 1-1/4 cups (300 mL) hot water. Add ice cream and stir until melted. Chill until partially set. Pull cake into pieces and add to first mixture. Spoon into sherbet glasses and chill well. Top with a fresh strawberry, if desired.
Serves 8

CANTALOUPE ICE

Mom used to make this when cantaloupes started ripening in our garden.

1	large ripe cantaloupe, peeled and seeded	1
1/3 cup	sifted icing sugar	75 mL
1 Tbsp	fresh lemon juice	15 mL

Peel, remove seeds and cut up cantaloupe. Place cantaloupe, icing sugar and lemon juice in blender and purée until fruit is finely crushed. Turn into an 8-inch (20 cm) metal pan. Cover and freeze until almost frozen, about 2 hours. Purée again. Return to pan. Cover and freeze until firm, at least 2 hours. About 10 minutes before serving, place in refrigerator to soften a bit.
Serves 4

PLAIN BAKED CUSTARD

This is a no-frills trip.

4	eggs	4
1/4 cup	sugar	50 mL
2-1/2 cups	milk	675 mL
1 tsp	vanilla extract	5 mL

In mixing bowl, beat eggs until foamy. Add sugar and 1/4 tsp (1 mL) salt; beat until thickened and lemon-colored. Add milk and vanilla; beat until smooth. Pour into greased 1-qt (1 L) casserole. Place casserole in pan containing 1 inch (2.5 cm) of hot water. Bake in preheated 300°F (140°C) oven for 1-1/4 hours.
Serves 4 to 6

EGGNOG CUSTARD

A simple treat, made on top of the stove.

2	eggs, slightly beaten	2
2 cups	dairy eggnog	500 mL
1/4 tsp	vanilla extract	1 mL
Pinch	nutmeg	Pinch

In bowl, stir eggs, eggnog and vanilla until well blended. Pour into 4 greased 6 oz (170 g) custard cups. Place on rack in large frying pan; sprinkle with nutmeg. Add boiling water to frying pan to cover bottom half of custard cups. Cover frying pan with lid or foil tent. Cook over low heat with water at a gentle simmer 12 to 15 minutes, or until a knife inserted near center of custard comes out clean. Center may look slightly loose. Serve at room temperature, or chilled.
Serves 4

GINGER BANANAS

Taste the way the flavors mingle.

1/2 cup	sugar	125 mL
1/4 cup	fresh lemon juice	50 mL
8	medium size very ripe bananas, peeled and sliced 1/4 inch (0.5 cm) thick	8
1 Tbsp	ground ginger	15 mL

In small saucepan, bring sugar, 1/2 cup (125 mL) water and lemon juice to a boil, stirring constantly until sugar dissolves. Cook 8 to 10 minutes. Meanwhile, arrange half the banana slices decoratively on a serving platter. Sprinkle with half the ginger. Top with remaining banana slices; top with remaining ginger. Pour syrup over bananas and chill before serving.
Serves 8

BANANAS NEW ORLEANS

Guess where I first ate this?

1	jar (12 oz/340 g) caramel ice cream topping	1
1/4 cup	banana liqueur	50 mL
6	small firm bananas	6
1 qt	vanilla ice cream	1 L

Combine banana liqueur and topping (and 1/2 tsp (2 mL) cinnamon if you have it handy) in a 12-inch (30 cm) frying pan. Peel bananas and cut in half lengthwise and crosswise. Add to topping mixture; heat thoroughly. Spoon bananas into 6 serving dishes. Top each serving with a scoop of ice cream and spoon sauce over ice cream.
Serves 6

COFFEE MALLOW

Coffee lovers will adore this.

22	large marshmallows	22
1 cup	strong black coffee	250 mL
1 cup	heavy cream, whipped	250 mL

In top of double boiler, combine marshmallows and coffee. Cook over hot water, stirring occasionally, until marshmallows are melted; cool. Fold in whipped cream. Turn into parfait glasses; freeze until firm.
Serves 6

CAFE PARÉE

Variation on the above theme.

1 cup	sugar	250 mL
3	egg whites, stiffly beaten	3
1 pint	whipping cream, whipped	500 mL
1/2 cup	strong black coffee	125 mL

In saucepan, boil together sugar and 1/2 cup (125 mL) water until syrup spins a thread 230°F (112°C) on candy thermometer). Add syrup gradually to stiffly beaten egg whites, beating all the time, until cold. Add coffee and three-quarters of the shipped cream. Mix well. Pour into mold and freeze until firm. Use the remaining whipped cream as a garnish.
Serves 6

FOUR-CUP FRUIT DESSERT

Some folks like to add a cup of flaked coconut to this and call it
"Five-Cup Fruit Dessert."

1 cup	drained pineapple chunks	250 mL
1 cup	drained mandarin oranges	250 mL
1 cup	miniature marshmallows	250 mL
1 cup	dairy sour cream	250 mL

In bowl, mix all ingredients. Refrigerate for 24 hours before
serving.
Serves 6 to 8

PEACH MELBA PARFAITS

Easy and elegant.

1 qt	vanilla ice cream	1 L
1/3 cup	Melba or raspberry sauce	75 mL
2 cups	peaches, sliced fresh or canned	500 mL
	or frozen thawed, drained	
	(plus extras for garnish)	
	Whipped cream	

In parfait glasses, layer ice cream, sauce and peaches. Garnish
with whipped cream and sliced peaches. Serve at once.
Serves 6

Miriam M. tells it: "Some years ago, during my 16th
month of postpartum depression, I decided to smarten up
and treat the family to a great dessert. The recipe called
for a topping of the packaged variety. I mixed and mixed
but the topping never became the consistency of whipped
cream. The next day, still vexed, I examined the directions on the packet again, and to my horror discovered
that I had not added the packet to the milk but had been
mixing straight milk with great determination!

CHANTILLY STRAWBERRIES

Lovely served at a bridal luncheon.

1 pint	strawberries	500 mL
2 Tbsp	orange-flavor liqueur	25 mL
1/2 cup	35% cream	125 mL
2 Tbsp	sugar	25 mL

Hull strawberries and reserve 4. Put remainder in blender or food processor and purée with liqueur. In bowl, whip cream with sugar until stiff. Fold in purée. Place in 4 dessert glasses. Slice 4 strawberries and use to garnish.
Serves 4

STRAWBERRY-ORANGE SORBET

Simple syrup is made by boiling equal amounts of water and sugar to syrup consistency, then cooling.

3 pints	strawberries, rinsed and hulled	1.5 L
1-3/4 cups	fresh orange juice	425 mL
1/4 cup	simple syrup	50 mL
1/4 cup	orange-flavor liqueur	50 mL

Place strawberries and orange juice in food processor with steel blade; process until smooth. This may be done in several batches for a small size processor. Add up to 1/4 cup (50 mL) simple syrup, to taste. Place in shallow dish or pan. Freeze until almost solid. Remove from freezer and spoon into processor; process until smooth and fluffy. Spoon into a 1 to 1-1/2-qt (1 to 1.5 L) mold and freeze solid. Remove about 15 minutes before serving and unmold onto serving plate. Refrigerate until serving time.
Serves about 10

Candy

Says: Don C.: "I decided to make it in a new enameled Dutch oven. I put in some shortening and set it on the burner on high. I guess it heated up faster than I thought. There was a tiny curl of vapor rising from the lid before I lifted it, and then the whole kitchen disappeared in a flash of orange as I stood in the middle of a fireball. You've no idea how much fire there is in just a little bit of shortening! Of course, I lost my eyebrows and the few hairs Nature hadn't already removed from the front of my scalp."

SPIRITED TRUFFLES

Absolutely elegant.

3 cups	semi-sweet chocolate pieces	750 mL
1	can (15 oz/426 g) sweetened condensed milk	1
3 Tbsp	bourbon	45 mL
1/2 cup	finely chopped walnuts	125 mL

In top of double boiler over hot (not boiling) water, melt chocolate pieces. Add condensed milk and stir until smooth. Remove from heat and add bourbon; chill 2 hours. Shape into 3/4-inch (2 cm) balls and roll in nuts. Chill until firm. Store at room temperature in tightly covered container. Flavor improves with age.
Makes 3 to 4 dozen

CHOCOLATE CRITTERS

Just like the expensive kind.

1 cup	pecan halves	250 mL
1/2 lb	soft caramels	250 g
1/4 cup	table cream	50 mL
4	squares unsweetened chocolate	4

On waxed paper-lined cookie sheet, place 3 pecan halves (1 for head; two for feet) for each critter. In a double boiler over hot water, melt the caramels with the cream. Cool for 10 minutes. Spoon caramel mixture over nuts and let cool 30 minutes. Melt chocolate over hot water in double boiler. Spread chocolate over caramel on nuts.
Makes about 24 critters

FOUR-CUP CANDY

A delicious confection.

1 cup	miniature marshmallows	250 mL
1 cup	chopped nuts	250 mL
1 cup	chopped dates	250 mL
1 cup	shredded coconut	250 mL

In top of double boiler over hot (not boiling) water, melt marshmallows. Remove from heat and mix in nuts and dates. Spread coconut on waxed paper and drop nut-date mixture by teaspoonfuls onto coconut. Roll in coconut and transfer to waxed paper-lined cookie sheet. Chill until firm.
Makes about 1-1/2 lbs (750 g)

ALMOND BALLS

A little expensive, but worth it.

1	can (8 oz/227 g) almond paste	1
2/3 cup	sifted icing sugar	150 mL
1/4 cup	light corn syrup	50 mL

In small mixing bowl, break almond paste into small pieces. Beat in sugar and corn syrup until well blended. Wrap about 1 tsp (5 mL) of the mixture around whole almond; shape into ball with palms of hands. Roll in colored sprinkles if you wish. Place in pleated foil candy cups if to be elegant about it.
Makes about 36 balls

As a bride, Emily R. was anxious to impress not only her husband but her first group of guests. Fudge sounded like a marvelous idea, so she made platters of it. Everything was ducky until everyone took a bite. It was then she discovered she had used chicken fat (stored in a margarine container) instead of margarine in the fudge. "I still hear about that, years later," she said.

CREAM PRALINES

Just like they make in New Orleans.

3 cups	sugar	750 mL
1 cup	table cream	250 mL
1/2 tsp	vanilla extract	2 mL
3 cups	pecans	750 mL

In heavy saucepan, boil together the sugar, cream, a pinch of salt and the vanilla for about 4 minutes, or until a little of the syrup forms a soft ball when it is dropped into cold water. Remove from heat, stir in pecans and immediately drop by teaspoonfuls onto waxed paper. Allow to cool and remove from waxed paper.
Makes about 1-1/2 lbs (750 g)

NUT-DATE KISSES

A nice way to get kissed.

6	egg whites, beaten stiff	6
1/2 lb	chopped nuts	250 g
2 cups	sugar	500 mL
1 lb	chopped dates	500 g

In medium bowl, combine ingredients. Drop by tablespoonfuls onto greased cookie sheets. Bake in preheated 325°F (160°C) oven about 30 minutes, or until light brown. Lower heat to 250°F (120°C) and bake for 10 more minutes.
Makes 60 to 70 kisses

COCONUT TRUFFLES

I am a member in good standing of CLUE (Coconut Lovers United Evermore).

1/2 cup	butter	125 mL
3 cups	sweetened shredded coconut	750 mL
2 cups	icing sugar	500 mL
6 oz	semisweet chocolate, melted	170 g

In large saucepan, melt butter. Remove from heat. Stir in coconut and icing sugar. Shape heaping teaspoonfuls of mixture into balls. Dip bottom of each ball into melted chocolate. Arrange chocolate side down on waxed paper-lined baking sheet. Refrigerate until firm, about 30 minutes. Serve chilled.
Makes about 3 dozen truffles

After concocting 50 bottles of sugarless root beer, Mary A. and her husband, Chuck, looked for a place to age it at a steady 85°F to 90°F. The oven of their gas stove seemed perfect, and for five days it aged there, fermenting and causing a lot of carbonation. Forgetting about the root beer, Mary turned the oven to 425°F to brown some dinner rolls. "We were talking in the livingroom about 10 minutes later," she says, "when the first explosion happened. I rushed into the kitchen and immediately did two things. One was smart and the other was stupid. The smart thing I did was turn off the oven. The stupid thing I did was open the oven door. The second explosion shot root beer and broken glass all the way into the livingroom. Luckily no one was hurt.

ORANGE-SUGARED WALNUTS OR PECANS

Store these in an airtight container.

1-1/2 cups	sugar	375 mL
3 Tbsp	frozen orange juice concentrate	45 mL
1/2 tsp	grated orange rind	2 mL
2 cups	pecan halves or walnut meats	500 mL

In medium heavy saucepan, combine sugar, 1/4 cup (50 mL) water and orange juice concentrate. Bring to a boil over medium heat, stirring constantly. Boil slowly without stirring to 240°F (118°C) on a candy thermometer, or until a small amount forms a semi-firm ball when dropped into a little cold water. Remove from heat. Add orange rind and pecan halves or walnuts. Stir until syrup begins to look cloudy. Drop by teaspoonfuls onto waxed paper in clusters. Cool.
Makes about 2 dozen clusters

"My mom, Beverly W., was in the mood for some candy," writes Lisa W. "So she decided to make the kind that starts with boiling sugar and water together. I guess she boiled it too long, because she wound up pouring it in the sink, where it quickly became so hard we had to remove it a chip at a time with a hammer and chisel. Not only that, but she had colored it with red food coloring, and it stained the sink terribly. We still tease her about that."

WHO? ME WORRY?

Methuselah ate what he found on his plate,
And never, as people do now,
Did he note the amount of the calorie count,
He ate it because it was chow.
He wasn't disturbed as at dinner he sat
Devouring a roast or a pie
To think it was lacking in glandular fat
Or a couple of vitamins shy.
He cheerfully chewed every species of food,
Untroubled by worries or fears
Lest his health might be hurt by some fancy dessert —
And he lived over nine hundred years.

Author Unknown

SPICE CHART

HOW MUCH SPICE TO USE: When trying a new idea, it is safest to start with 1/4 tsp (1 mL) of spice (excepting the red pepper spices) to a pint (500 mL) of sauce, soup or vegetable or a pound (500 g) of meat, fish or fowl.

SPICE	APPETIZER	SOUP	MEAT and EGGS	FISH and POULTRY
ALLSPICE	Cocktail Meatballs	Pot au Feu	Ham-Steak	Oyster Stew
BASIL	Cheese-Stuffed Celery	Manhattan Clam Chowder	Ragout of Beef	Shrimp Creole
BAY LEAF	Pickled Beets	Vegetable	Lamb Stew	Simmered Chicken
CARAWAY Seed	Mild Cheese Spreads		Sauerbraten	
CINNAMON	Cranberry Juice	Fruit	Pork Chops	Sweet and Sour Fish
CAYENNE	Deviled Eggs	Oyster Stew	Barbecued Beef	Poached Salmon Hollandaise
CELERY Salt and Seed	Ham Spread (Salt)	Cream of Celery (Seed)	Meat Loaf (Seed)	Chicken Croquettes (Salt)
CHERVIL	Fish Dips	Cream	Omelet	Chicken Sauté
CHILI Powder	Seafood Cocktail Sauce	Pepper Pot	Chili con Carne	Arroz con Pollo
CLOVES	Fruit Punch	Mulligatawney	Boiled Tongue	Baked Fish
CURRY Powder	Curried Shrimp	Cream of Mushroom	Curry of Lamb	Chicken Hash
DILL Seed	Cottage Cheese	Split Pea	Grilled Lamb Steak	Drawn Butter for Shellfish
GARLIC Salt or Instant Minced	Clam Dip	Vegetable	Roast Lamb	Bouillabaisse
GINGER	Broiled Grapefruit	Bean	Dust lightly over Steak	Roast Chicken
MACE	Quiche Lorraine	Petite Marmite	Veal Fricassee	Fish Stew
MARJORAM	Fruit Punch Cup	Onion	Roast Lamb	Salmon Loaf
MINT	Fruit Cup	Sprinkle over Split Pea	Veal Roast	Cold Fish
MUSTARD Powdered Dry	Ham Spread	Lobster Bisque	Virginia Ham	Deviled Crab
NUTMEG	Chopped Oysters	Cream DuBarry	Salisbury Steak	Southern Fried Chicken
ONION Powder, Salt, Flakes and Instant Minced Onion	Avocado Spread (Powder)	Consommés (Flakes)	Meat Loaf (Instant Minced Onion)	Fried Shrimp (Salt)
OREGANO	Sharp Cheese Spread	Beef	Swiss Steak	Court Bouillon
PAPRIKA	Creamed Seafood	Cream	Hungarian Goulash	Oven Fried Chicken
PARSLEY Flakes	Cheese Balls	Cream of Asparagus	Irish Lamb Stew	Broiled Mackerel
ROSEMARY	Deviled Eggs	Mock Turtle	Lamb Loaf	Chicken à la King
SAGE	Cheese Spreads	Consommé	Cold Roast Beef	Poultry Stuffing
SAVORY	Liver Paste	Lentil	Scrambled Eggs	Chicken Loaf
TARRAGON	Mushrooms à la Greque	Snap Bean	Marinated Lamb or Beef	Lobster
THYME	Artichokes	Clam Chowder	Use sparingly in Fricassees	Poultry Stuffing

SPICE	SAUCES	VEGETABLES	SALAD and DRESSING	DESSERTS
ALLSPICE	Barbecue	Eggplant Creole	Cottage Cheese Dressing	Apple Tapioca Pudding
BASIL	Spaghetti	Stewed Tomatoes	Russian Dressing	
BAY LEAF	Bordelaise	Boiled New Potatoes	Tomato Juice Dressing	
CARAWAY Seed	Beef à la Mode Sauce	Cabbage Wedges		
CINNAMON	Butter Sauce for Squash	Sweet Potato Croquettes	Stewed Fruit Salad	Chocolate Pudding
CAYENNE	Bearnaise	Cooked Greens	Tuna Fish Salad	
CELERY Salt and Seed	Celery Sauce (Seed)	Cauliflower (Salt)	Coleslaw (Seed)	
CHERVIL	Vegetable Sauce	Peas Francaise	Caesar Salad	
CHILI Powder	Meat Gravy	Corn Mexicali	Chili French Dressing	
CLOVES	Sauce Madeira	Candied Sweet Potatoes		Stewed Pears
CURRY Powder	Orientale or Indienne	Creamed Vegetables	Curried Mayonnaise	
DILL Seed	Dill Sauce for Fish or Chicken	Peas and Carrots	Sour Cream Dressing	
GARLIC Salt or Instant Minced	Garlic Butter	Egg and Tomato Casserole	Tomato and Cucumber Salad	
GINGER	Cocktail	Buttered Beets	Cream Dressing for Ginger Pears	Stewed Dried Fruits
MACE	Creole	Succotash	Fruit Salad	Cottage Pudding
MARJORAM	Brown	Eggplant	Mixed Green Salad	
MINT	Lamb	Green Peas	Cottage Cheese Salad	Ambrosia
MUSTARD Powdered Dry	Cream Sauce for Fish	Baked Beans	Egg Salad	Gingerbread Cookies
NUTMEG	Mushroom	Glazed Carrots	Sweet Salad Dressing	Sprinkle over Vanilla Ice Cream
ONION Powder, Salt, Flakes and Instant Minced Onion	Tomato (Powder)	Broiled Tomatoes (Salt)	Vinaigrette Dressing (Instant Minced Onion)	
OREGANO	Spaghetti	Boiled Onions	Seafood	
PAPRIKA	Paprika Cream	Baked Potato	Coleslaw	
PARSLEY Flakes	Chasseur	French Fried Potatoes	Tossed Green Salad	
ROSEMARY	Cheese	Sautéed Mushrooms	Meat Salad	
SAGE	Duck	Brussels Sprouts	Herbed French Dressing	
SAVORY	Fish	Beets	Red Kidney Bean Salad	
TARRAGON	Green	Buttered Broccoli	Chicken Salad	
THYME	Bordelaise	Lightly on Sautéed Mushrooms	Tomato Aspic	

COURTESY AMERICAN SPICE TRADE ASSOCIATION

INDEX